Wordplaygrounds

Wordplaygrounds

Reading, Writing, and Performing Poetry in the English Classroom

John S. O'Connor
New Trier High School, Winnetka, Illinois

National Council of Teachers of English
1111 W. Kenyon Road, Urbana, Illinois 61801-1096

Staff Editor: Bonny Graham
Interior Design: Doug Burnett
Cover Design: Pat Mayer

NCTE Stock Number: 58196

Library of Congress Cataloging-in-Publication Data
O'Connor, John S.
  Wordplaygrounds : reading, writing, and performing poetry in the English
classroom / John S. O'Connor.
    p. cm.
  Includes bibliographical references.
  ISBN 0-8141-5819-6 (pbk)
  1. Poetry—Study and teaching (Middle school)—United States.
2. Poetry—Study and teaching (Secondary)—United States. 3. Creative
writing (Middle school) 4. Oral interpretation of poetry. 5. Creative
writing (Secondary) I. Title.
  LB1576.O29 2004

                                                          2004017792

With love and gratitude to Eleni, Alison, and Ted.

Permission Acknowledgments

Contents

Acknowledgments

Worldplaygrounds has been the most ambitious and most satisfying collaboration of my professional life. I am deeply indebted to many people who offered direct and indirect assistance over the past five years I have spent working on this book. I need to single out a number of people who were particularly instrumental in the formulation and execution of this book.

First, I am thankful to all of the poets and performers who generously shared their time and talents in my classrooms. These artists made me a better teacher through their example and their instruction.

I am incredibly grateful to and thankful for the help of Hilary Strang, Betsy Edgerton, and Kate Duvall, great readers and great friends. Each read the book carefully and generously—sometimes wading through multiple drafts of the same chapter—to make the book much stronger than it would otherwise have been.

On the NCTE front, I am grateful for the faith that Michael Greer and Pete Feely showed in an ambitious but sketchy proposal five years ago. The superb editorial staff—Tom Tiller, Kurt Austin, and Bonny Graham—have shepherded this book through many stages and evolutions into a much more focused and finished project.

I am thankful to the University of Chicago Laboratory Schools for allowing me the creative freedom to try out new ideas in class after class. The faculty also taught me a great deal, and I am lucky to have had such wonderful collaborators.

In regard to the section on performance, I am very grateful for the help of a pair of brilliant middle school drama teachers at the Lab Schools, Lisa and John Biser. They generously allowed me to use their trio of performance terms (*punch, pause,* and *color*), which I adapted in Chapters 10 through 12. I learned a great deal from them, and from students they taught, and hope I have extended their work in some new and interesting ways.

Most of all, this book would not be possible without the support of my family. My children, Alison and Ted, continue to teach me how important poetry is to their and our lives. My wife, Eleni, has always had more confidence in me than I have in myself. She introduced me to many of the poems and ideas in this book, and she read and discussed many of the ideas critically and lovingly.

Finally, I owe a great deal to all of my students, past and present. I often say (as if jokingly, but it's embarrassingly true), "Nearly all of my good ideas in class come from my students." Reading over hundreds of student poems over the past dozen or so years has helped me realize just how proud I am to call myself a teacher and just how lucky I am to have been touched by so many wonderful people.

1 Everyday Poets

"Poetry—merely whispering its name frightens everyone away" (43), says former Poet Laureate Rita Dove. Poetry frightens many of my students because it conjures up images of the impossibly distant past—like speaking Babylonian or medieval tournament jousting—not their immediate lives right here, right now.

But poetry is not a past-tense activity. Poetry is around us all the time—why, right now it's in this room in what we see, hear, taste, touch, and smell; it's on the radio in song lyrics and raps; it's on the playground in jump rope chants and basketball trash talk; it's in everyday conversations, in the things that go unsaid and in the things we don't yet have the words to say. Poetry is already in our lives, and poetry can help us more fully participate in our own lives and in the lives of others.

While I know that only the rare student will aspire to become a professional poet or a career writer, I want my students to see their writing as part of their lives, not an end in itself. To do this, we must eliminate, in John Dewey's words, "the gap between the child's experience and the various forms of subject matter that make up the course of study" (*Selected* 344). Poetry writing allows their experiences *to be* the course of study.

Poetry instruction in schools often feels artificial, consisting of little more than gimmicky exercises that have no audience but the teacher and no life outside the classroom. Such formulaic exercises have little to do with poetry because they have little to do with life. As Louise Rosenblatt has argued, literature needs to be "rescued from its diminished status as a body of subject matter, and offered as a mode of personal life experience" (x).

In this book, I present some ways teachers can use students' personal life experiences to (1) help students become less afraid and more comfortable with poetry and (2) help students see how poetry writing and performance connect to their lives and how poetry can enrich their lives.

In My Life

My students' attitude toward poetry as something distant and frightening is an attitude I know well. Their feelings parallel my own experiences with poetry.

I loved nursery rhymes as a child. I especially loved the Dr. Seuss books. I remember playing rhyming games with my mother as we walked home from Mayfair Park, and trying out primitive puns on my brother's and sisters' names as a youngest child's desperate last defense. I loved listening to animal poems in elementary school and then crawling around on the floor to act out the words.

Then poetry abruptly stopped for me. I'm not saying I never heard a teacher read a poem again in a classroom. The only thing I remember about the rest of my school life is that it all happened so fast. I didn't really get a good look at it.

Aside from a required Shakespeare class, I almost managed to avoid taking a single poetry class throughout college and graduate school. The one notable exception was a class called Anglo-Irish Literature taught by Professor F. X. Kinahan, a fiery, rotund Irishman with a big red beard and a flair for the dramatic. I loved reading Yeats, and I especially loved to hear Mr. Kinahan read Yeats. His readings were spectacular—little theater pieces, really. Like the rest of the class, I was enthralled by his performances and in awe of his delivery, the way he'd linger over a line as though he were reading from his own personal musical score: "Red Rose, proud Rose, sad Rose of all my days." I believed, at the time, that he had The Gift (and not the Gift of the Gab, which he also had), the innate ability to read, understand, and perform poetry. I was equally convinced that I did not.

Otherwise, I steered clear of poetry classes. I remember being terrified when a friend tried to talk me into signing up for a poetry writing class. The very idea of writing a poem seemed completely foreign to me. (I had never even seen a Grecian urn until I visited my wife Eleni's house before our marriage.) And, if I had actually tried my hand at writing a poem, I certainly would have kept it quiet. Nobody talks about poetry, do they?

Poetry was simply not for me, I thought, and I held this view for at least the first ten years of my teaching career. I thought poetry should be taught by people like Patricia, a colleague during my first year of high school teaching, which was in a big suburban public school. Pat was sort of an Earth Mother: dangling earrings, bright floral scarves, and an astonishing array of clothing homespun by native peoples. She had founded the school's literary magazine, *The Egg*. While my students pored over texts in their seats, Pat's students practiced "creative movement" exercises and yoga positions; while we discussed and debated evidence, they learned new breathing techniques.

Like many teachers, I used poetry only to meet certain curricular demands, or if I was pressed for time. The poems my students wrote were often formulaic gimmicks found in textbooks: acrostic and anagram poems, limericks, and haiku taught in the rigid 5-7-5 syllable mode. My students were as terrified as I was to try their hands at "real poetry."

It's not hard to find the source of this fear. I'm looking at a literature textbook right now that has reprinted Shakespeare's Sonnet 18 with an activity below: "A sonnet is a 14-line poem written in iambic pentameter. Try one of your own." Reading a prompt like this, who wouldn't conclude that poetry is reserved for geniuses?

Inspired by school visits from poets such as Luis Rodriguez and Naomi Shihab Nye, however, I started to read more contemporary poetry. The immediacy of poets reading their own work was exciting. I decided to read whatever I liked, to let the poets I enjoyed reading recommend other poets to read, and never to apologize for putting aside a poem I didn't like or understand.

Like many of my students, I also listened to contemporary music. (I play the guitar and used to select the music for a folk music radio show.) I especially loved songwriting with thoughtful lyrics: Bob Dylan, Melissa Etheridge, Ira Gershwin, Chuck D, Dave Frishberg. So I decided (as I knew many teachers had before me) to use pop songs as a means of understanding poems. I'll never forget how a student named Buddy—who had very little interest in school—created a slide show of his own photographs to illustrate the differences between Paul Simon's "The Sound of Silence" and a Gwendolyn Brooks poem about urban Chicago. Or how Angel—"a gangbanger who'll never graduate," I'd been told—compared generational attitudes toward fathers in Dylan Thomas's "Youth Calls to Age" with a rap song by Sir Mix-a-Lot. I felt like I was really on to something: My students had a great deal to say and a desperate urge to express themselves. Poetry gave them the voice to do this.

I read everything on teaching poetry I could find. I especially liked Kenneth Koch's books (such as *Rose, Where Did You Get That Red?*; *Wishes, Lies and Dreams*; and *Sleeping on the Wing*, with Kate Farrell) and began having my students write poems in imitation of famous poets. Having a good model to follow is as effective in writing poems as it is for every other kind of writing. But writing "in the style of" another poet is necessarily limiting. Many books left me frustrated by their vague directions ("Write about a special dream") or suggestions that seemed to overdetermine the resulting poem ("Write a poem about a physical trait of yours you wish you could change"). The variety and creativity of my students' work always reminds me how important it is to give students a range of models (moods, forms, ideas) for each poem assignment so that they have a chance to write about something they are passionate about even if it means leaving the models behind.

One day, when I told the class they'd have fun writing their next poem (a poem requiring them to interview a friend), a student said, "If it's so much fun, you do it." I did, and have tried every assignment I have given since. Writing poems with the class has helped me understand difficulties inherent in the assignment. It also creates tremendous trust with my students, who see me working alongside them. If it's worth my time, it must be worth theirs, they seem to say. More than that, I really have fun writing these poems with my students—the kind of fun I had as a boy, playing alongside Dr. Seuss. And I am very proud of some of what I have written, even if not all of my poems are entirely successful.

Pride is clear in what my students write too. At the end of the year, they routinely report that, of all the writing they do, they are most proud of a single poem they have written. By writing poems, my students have not only studied literature, but they have also created it. And, at the end of the day, their feeling of accomplishment is what I am most proud of.

Teaching Poetry

> I don't write poems. Actually, I used to write poems, but I can't write anymore. (I've tried.) You'd have to be a wizard or something, and magic is something I'm kind of short on these days!
>
> —grade 10 student

This student was responding to a questionnaire I passed out on the first day of school. One of my first goals every year is to demystify poetry because this student, like many of my students, enters the class convinced she lacks the requisite capacity for literary wizardry. Yet her writing does possess a sort of magic. She uses a metaphor (though interestingly she changes the pronoun from "I" to "you" in describing the hypothetical word wizard). Also, she uses a figure of speech in imagining that an abstract quality like magic can be something she could run out of. And yet she is scared by poetry.

To minimize my students' fears, I begin my classes by asking students to play around with words. As poet Donald Hall says, "All poets start from love of words and wordplay" (69). My initial poetry writing exercises (starting in Chapter 2) begin with everyday words and phrases: ice cream brands, album titles, common objects found around the house.

These activities are designed to demystify poetry and to build confidence.

These early exercises are shorter (single-word lines, relatively simple lists) than later assignments for several reasons. Students find short assignments less daunting, and everyone can write and have fun with these poem exercises. Also, very short poems ensure immediate feedback. With everyone's short poems on the board, we can ask specific questions together: Why start with that word? What if you switched these two words? Students spontaneously revise and rearrange on the spot.

Since all of the exercises that follow build on previous assignments, this book can be used to guide a full unit of poetry; however, the exercises also work independently as discrete lessons. Depending on students' ages and abilities, teachers can choose the exercises that best fit their curricula. In my classes, as students grow more confident I gradually ask them to write longer, more complicated poems. These poems will be less intimidating because students can use skills they have accumulated from earlier exercises and because we work from model poems written by professional poets and by fellow students alike.

Using Models

Most of the poetry exercises in this book are derived from patterns I've noticed in poems I love. The "sliding doors" poem in Chapter 7, for example, comes from Billy Collins's "I Go Back to the House for a Book" and from David Hernandez's "Sun-Times." The speaker in Collins's poem reflects on how his life is different, richer, because of a decisive action he took. Hernandez's hilarious poem shows the consequences of *not* acting. This speaker averts a nuclear holocaust and saves the world by deciding against stealing his neighbor's newspaper.

I give several student models alongside the professional models with each assignment. Here I agree with Joseph Tsujimoto, who says that "giving students many examples, by both students and adults, can actually encourage original poetry" (10). Offering diverse models suggests a greater number of possibilities to students, forces them to negotiate which forms and patterns will help them best convey their thoughts, and eliminates the notion that there is somehow a "right answer," a model to be followed exactly. (Note: Most of the student models in this book come from my English classes, grades 8–12, at the University of Chicago Lab Schools. I have also included some samples from elementary school and junior high poetry classes I have taught during the summer. These classes included students from public and private schools throughout Chicago. I do not usually tell my students the ages of the authors—unless they ask—and I have used these models in classes and workshops with students who have ranged in age from eight to eighty.)

The Teacher as Coach

Because I want students to see poetry as something useful and vital in their lives outside of school, I see my role as that of a coach rather than a critic. I stand on the sidelines with students—not across the desk from them—helping them consider the best strategies for reaching their various audiences and writing aims. Since I am not necessarily their intended reader, I am not the final arbiter of whether a poem is effective; however, I'm happy to tell students what I think of the choices they've made and how successfully their poem achieves their desired effects. I try to phrase suggestions as questions: Can you say this in fewer words? Is it necessary to repeat this idea here? Why did you choose to switch tenses in the second stanza? Will the lack of punctuation here confuse your readers?

I don't assign letter grades to poems, but this is not because I don't believe that poems can be judged. Rather, I mark poems with a +, a √, or a √- in terms of their *completeness.* Rather than say, "Yes, this is a great poem" or "No, this one isn't any good," I say, "Great job! This poem fully completes the assignment and was lots of fun to read," or "This is a good start, but the second section needs to be developed more fully. Let's revise this together."

Revision

I allow students to revise their poems as many times as they like. This minimizes their fears of "making mistakes," and it encourages kids to take risks, to try new ways of using language. Even students who rarely revise write more boldly knowing the safety net of revision hangs beneath them. (Note: I'll briefly outline my feelings toward revision here, but I offer a longer discussion and much more specific classroom strategies in Chapter 9.)

Poet Mary Oliver says she usually has to "revise through forty or fifty drafts of a poem before [she] begins to feel content with it. Other poets take longer" (111). While I confess I don't usually revise my own drafts fifty times, I have never written anything that has not undergone substantial revision after the initial draft. I tell my students about the time I had to rewrite a five-word haiku twice before a literary editor accepted the poem. Students deserve the same opportunity to keep shaping a piece until they and their readers are satisfied with it. When I mention this revision policy to teachers, they sometimes gasp: "You mean every student can revise everything as often as they want?" Yes, but the number of takers is *very* small, partly because my students don't want to increase their own workload, and partly because I insist on meeting briefly with students to find out why they are interested in revising.

If a student wants to revise merely to fulfill the assignment, I might have him or her revise a portion of the poem ("Rewrite two sensory descriptions," for example, or "See if you can rewrite the first stanza using half the number of words"). If, however, the student poet is genuinely interested in revising the poem for his or her own sake (like the girl last year who said she wanted to keep writing to find out why her grandmother's music box mattered so much to her), I am happy to look at multiple drafts. It is not common for students to be so intrinsically motivated. Many students consider substantial revision only when they are preparing a final draft for publication. For this reason, our writing assignments culminate in publishing classroom collections as well as books written by individual authors.

Author-izing Students

Creating books of poems is a great way for students to see their work in new ways and a great way to help students see themselves as poets. My students publish collective "class books," and individual books as well. Both kinds of publishing help to achieve Dewey's unifying aim of education: "the growth of the child in the direction of social capacity and service, and his more vital union with life" (*Selected* 80). In other words, publishing books lets students do the work of professional writers and also face the same challenges these writers face.

In compiling class books, it is essential that everyone submit the same number of poems, or perhaps the same number of pages, since the length of poems varies dramatically. This page limitation forces students to review their body of work and to choose those poems suitable for a more general audience. Writing books helps to turn the classroom into a community of writers, and it gives students with different skills— word processing, layout, drawing—a special chance to excel.

Writing individual books has become another hugely important part of my course. For years I asked students to maintain writing portfolios, file folders stuffed with multiple revisions of poems. Then one year an eleventh-grade student whose father had died during the middle of our poetry unit showed me how to use these folders in a more significant way. Although this boy missed a lot of school, he wrote a great deal during this time, and he found poetry to be an important release for his new and overwhelming feelings. When he turned in all his missing work, he had entitled his folder "Reflections in a Cracked Mirror," and he wrote a letter of introduction explaining the source of some of the poems and a rationale for the order in which he had placed them. This student showed me how the process of collecting poems could imitate the work professional poets do: selecting and ordering poems, titling their collections, explaining their sources, and offering a statement of introduction. Perhaps most important, this project gives students a chance to revisit their work, retrace their thoughts over an extended creative period, and measure their growth as writers. Students are often amazed at the topics they've chosen to return to: a grandmother, a favorite pet, friendships, dreams.

My students do not have to copy and bind these books, but their sense of accomplishment is great nonetheless. The books are a testament to the work they have done, not only the written work but also the work of discovering themselves and the world around them more fully. Their pride is as clear on their faces as it is in their writing.

At one point, several students started an online journal called *The Paper Tango*. The journal, as the students described it, encouraged submissions from all students—they even solicited electronic manuscripts from students at other schools. Their goal was to reach a wider audience, and they encouraged comments on any and all poems they posted. The only stipulation they made was that only a reader who had submitted a poem could comment on the poetry of others. They also went out of their way to let readers know that "all work posted on *The Paper Tango* is work in progress." They emphasized writing as a process and saw poetry as a means of building a larger community of writers and sharing their ideas with an audience outside the classroom.

Poetry and Performance

Poetry is too often taught as a solipsistic act: something to be done in private, like keeping a secret diary, with no regard for an audience beyond the poet. As Stanley Kunitz has pointed out, however, poetry "must be felt to be understood, and before it can be felt it must be heard. Poets listen for their poems, and we, as readers, must listen in turn. If we listen hard enough, who knows? We too may break into dance" (qtd. in Janeczko 74). Performing poetry offers students the opportunity to celebrate language through a wide range of media, including the instrument of their own voices.

This celebration of language is what Dana Gioia urges in his book *Can Poetry Matter? Essays on Poetry and American Culture:*

> The sheer joy of the art must be emphasized. The pleasure of poetry is what first attracts children to poetry, the sensual excitement of speaking and hearing the words of the poem. Performance was also the teaching technique that kept poetry vital for centuries. Perhaps it holds the key to poetry's future. (23)

Much of the excitement and vitality in my classes comes when students discover their own reading voices and reinvent their own language in order to communicate their most important ideas and feelings.

Students need as much positive feedback and encouragement when reading poems as they do when writing poems. So we applaud every reading. Applause goes a long way toward creating a community of writers and reminds students they are not merely writing poems for class. They have a larger audience (and an adoring public!).

In my classes, each poem is read twice, once by the author and then by a classmate. Students learn about their own poems through the differences in the readings—changes in tone, different ways of reading lines, punctuation. It is important to move outside the classroom as well. At most poetry readings, the audience sits quietly for thirty minutes or an hour and applauds only at the end. The audience is expected to attend with silent reverence, as though at a church service. (This may explain why some poetry readings—and some church services—are so poorly attended!) *Wordplaygrounds* ends, as my classes do, with suggestions for organizing public readings, dramatizing poems, and integrating poetry with other disciplines.

The school day is so fragmented that it is easy to forget how isolated our classes can become and how chaotic and random much of our students' learning must seem to them. Dewey argued that "school as a whole is [to be] related to life as a whole" (*Selected* 80). We need to find ways of connecting disciplines and working on common rather than competing academic timetables. Finding common areas of interest and study will not only help our students make more sense of their learning but also help us all remember why our work matters so much. My students learn quickly that poetry is not something foreign to their experience; it *is* their experience. Poetry offers students the opportunity to explore their language, their world, and themselves more deeply than they otherwise would. Perhaps most important, writing and performing poetry help my students see that they are not just studying literature, they are also creating it.

Poetry, my students come to understand, is not something to fear, but rather an invitation to participate fully in our everyday lives. Here, for example, is the advice of one student who entered the class convinced he "could not ever write a poem":

Don't Be Afraid

Writing poetry
Is not as daunting as it sounds.
All you have to have done
To write poetry
Is to have lived.

I'm alive,
So I can write poetry.
Anyone reading this is presumably alive;
Therefore, you too
Are capable of writing poetry.

Once you establish
That you are, in fact, alive,
Your poetry may be governed
By your mood. If you're hungry,
For example, there's an excellent chance
That your poem will reflect your hunger.

Some choose to be coy with their meanings
And highfalutin' with their language
("Bubbles in an IV loitering" or
 "Museums mark their bodies down")

This is okay sometimes,
But you don't want to hide
Your poem's meaning
From the reader altogether.

Do you understand now
Why writing poetry is not as hard
As you thought?

Proof of life, mood, language:
Three simple steps
And your poetry
Will flow
Like water.

—Rob, grade 10

2 Preparing the Palette

What You Need for Painting
From a letter by Renoir

THE PALETTE

Flake white	*Rose madder*
Chrome yellow	*Cobalt blue*
Naples yellow	*Ultramarine blue*
Yellow ocher	*Emerald green*
Raw umber	*Ivory black*
Venetian red	*Raw sienna*
French vermilion	*Viridian green*
Madder lake	*White lead*

DON'T FORGET
Palette knife
Scraping knife
Essence of turpentine

BRUSHES?
Pointed marten-hair brushes
Flat hog-hair brushes
Indifference to everything except your canvas.
The ability to work like a locomotive.
An iron will.

—Raymond Carver

Through early exercises, I hope to help students see that poetry often takes as its subject ordinary objects from the everyday world. Even more important, I want students to see that they already possess palettes of their own—their own words and experiences—from which they can write their own poems.

Raymond Carver's "What You Need for Painting"—a list poem plucked from a letter by the painter Auguste Renoir—serves as good advice for writing poems. Writing also demands specificity, revision, and concentration. Carver's poem is also a good introductory poem because it seems so easy. It doesn't rhyme. There is not a single complete sentence in the poem. One girl said, "Big deal. All he had to do was open a 128-pack of crayons." Neither Renoir nor Carver, however, would be satisfied by a different list of colors, say, "blue, red, pink, orange, yellow." Artists are interested in exactitude—colors and words that look, sound, and feel just right. "The difference between the almost right word and the right word," Mark Twain said, "is the difference between the lightning bug and the lightning." I like the idea of writing one-word-per-line list poems because it allows students to see the importance of individual words, and because these exercises ensure an early taste of success for everyone in the class.

Word Warm-ups

Most singers would never dream of performing without vocalizing, or warming up their voices. Likewise, word warm-up exercises can loosen students' tongues and their imaginations. In my classes, I often have kids make lists in a circle as a five-minute warm-up activity before each lesson. They name foods they've never tried, animals they wish they could have as pets, places they'd like to visit. Often I can tailor the lists to the lesson at hand. Students might name words that start with the same letter (to reinforce alliteration); words that contain a common vowel sound (to reinforce assonance); gerunds or participles (to reinforce parallel parts of speech); words that start with the same letter that ended the previous word. (My students and I once played this with song and movie titles for five solid hours on a bus trip back from downstate Illinois.)

This quick-paced round-robin sharing ensures that every student speaks early on in the class, and it gives each student the chance to play with language in new and unexpected ways.

Word Association Poems

The simplest list poems we write are word association poems. My students and I love to play a word association game in which they must say a word suggested by the word before it. The only ground rules are that the words must be connected somehow and that the connection must be understandable to the rest of the class. So the word *run* might be followed by *score, home, race,* or *stocking.* I allow students to help the class see connections, but if the speaker cannot convince the class of the connection, he or she must change the word.

Students enjoy playing this game as a class, and they are as surprised as they are proud when I call their finished chains "poems." These poems are, perhaps, not very sophisticated, but students have strung together words in a meaningful fashion, and they've had fun and success using language in a new way. The only additional rule I add, when I have students write their own word association poems, is that the last word must return to the first. This gives the whole poem greater shape. Here are two lists developed by middle school students:

Baseball	Horse
glove	racing
lady	car
dance	trunk
Cinderella	elephant
pumpkin	zoo
Halloween	penguins
mask	polar
catcher	opposites
baseball.	not
	tie
	collar
	leash
	dog
	food
	horse

I encourage students to create surprising links between lines, such as the leap from a glove used by a ball player to a formal garment worn by a lady, or the leap from a polar climate to polar opposites. Students love writing word association poems both alone and with friends. Many students keep writing these poems throughout the year and bring them in to share with the class.

I encourage students to keep a journal of new and interesting words and phrases, and to play around with new chains of words. It's helpful for students to see that journal entries don't need to take any particular form. A single word might be an entry. I love the idea of word-tickets that Susan Wooldridge writes of in *Poemcrazy*. She and her students tape interesting words and combinations of words on the back of carnival tickets that say "Admit One." Interesting and surprising words really are like admission tickets, allowing readers to join us in our own wordplaygrounds.

List Poems

I assign the topics of these early list poems. (Students can generate their own lists later.) I have used ice-cream flavors, movie titles, the Yellow

Pages, breakfast cereals, book titles, car models—any pool of words with very specific and interesting connotations. Here is a quick list of book titles I spot on the shelf next to me:

White Pine

West Wind

Tracks

Fresh Scent

The Beak of the Finch

The Siege

The Flowering Tree

Love Medicine

The Old Forest

This list begins to tell an interesting story—of a hunt? The struggle for survival? I chose not to include every title on the shelf. I avoided titles such as *Nichomachean Ethics, Neurobiology,* and *The Forsyte Saga,* for example. Remember Renoir's scraping knife?

Here are a couple of list poems students wrote:

[with song titles]
Love Letters

In dreams
Night streets
Driving sideways
Final miles
Timesteps
Fifty years after the fair
I float alone
The nightingale
Into the night
       —John, grade 12

[with perfumes]
Heaven

Soul mates
Sand and Sable
So pink
Candied melon
Modern
Om
       —Jordann, grade 12

[with board games]
Pretty, Pretty Princess

Girl Talk
Scrabble
Taboo
Life
Risk

[with song titles]
Crazy Love

God must have spent a little
   more time on you
Because you loved me
Like I love you
The two of us

Don't Wake Daddy
Sorry
    —Ari, grade 10

Can't fight the moonlight.
Sometimes you drive me crazy
But I do love you,
Truly, madly, deeply.
I can't let you go.
    —Priyanka, grade 9

One day during a summer poetry class in the junior high, students pleaded for an ice-cream break. I reminded them of Czeslaw Milosz's line: "Poetry makes bread unnecessary." To which they replied, "Sure, bread. But notice he didn't say anything about ice cream!" I broke down and bought them Popsicles, but only after they, as a class, wrote this list, which they chanted as a jump rope rhyme:

Good Humor

Chocolate Chip Cookie Dough
Chocolate Chip Sandwich
Chocolate Mocha
Chocolate Walnut
Chocolate Chocolate Fudge
Chunky Monkey
King Cone
Mississippi Mud
Superman
Smiley Face
Triple. Thick. Milk. Shake.
Tweety Bird
Toasted Almond
Sponge Bob Square Pants
Word.
    —class of fifth to eighth graders

While this is not an altogether successful poem, the class was beginning to use specific language in interesting ways. Class members later sorted themselves by common sounds and then performed the poem together, playing up the paired sounds and having fun with each line. Students began to create interesting combinations of sounds and to use the everyday world around them.

These early exercises help students pay attention to sound and connotation. It is important that students hear the connotative power of specificity. The poet Reginald Gibbons asks students to create language hierarchies from metonym (the language of broad categories, such as birds) to hyponym (the language of specific subcategories, such as American bald eagle) in order to get students to appreciate specificity. When I've had students create simple hierarchies, I've found it helpful to use reference books such as *Descriptionary, The Order of Things,* and various technical manuals (music, electronics, architecture) that list specific terminology for thousands of common objects. As a quick exercise, then, a student might write a list such as this: fruit, hesperidium, citrus, orange, blood orange. I want students to see the connotative richness of *blood oranges* or *summer squash* that words like *fruits* and *vegetables* lack.

Map Poems

"Map" is an elaborate list that relishes the sounds and specificity of its words:

A Map of Dodge County, Wisconsin
for Jane Eggert

Elk horns, beaver teeth, bell jars, bauxite; cap pistols, pin cushions, air rifles, sacks of dice; pewter doves and tin lovebirds, plaster polar bears and ceramic moose; potato mashers, rolling pins, canning jars, ladles; rococo salvers and baroque cornucopias; shoe trees, cheese wheels, antique beakers of Lash's bitters; margarita glasses stolen from Chi-Chi's; Olde Copenhagen candy bowls in cyanine, verbena, sienna, and spruce; salt and pepper shakers shaped like Li'l Black Sambo; a Queen Victoria tea service and the Joan Baez songbook; geodesic ashtrays from the New York World's Fair; a smiling Air India kewpie panjandrum; a Bob Johnson hand-carved "Bluebill Drake"; an *Atlas of Norse Myth and Icelandic Sagas;* a guide to Wisconsin's favorite trade in the souvenir taps and banners and trays from Hamm's and Pabst and Miller and Blatz; a map of Dodge County in the vintage collections of brown glass bottles embossed with the totem and heraldic crests of the local burghers' vanished brews: White Cap, North Star, Gold Label, Falls City; Zeigler's, Kurth's, Grat's, Jung's; Alps Brau and Fox DeLuxe, Holiday and Munchner; Hauenstein, Pioneer, Chief Oshkosh, Oconto.

— Campbell McGrath

After I have students read this poem, I ask them to write maps of defined spaces in their lives—their towns, their bedrooms, their basements, their garages—any place filled with interesting objects and names. Here is one student's response:

Bedroom Cartography

White and black photographs
And music from the motion picture *Magnolia*,
A One and a Two: Joel and Ethan, *Harold and Maude*, and *Twin Peaks.*
A cardboard skull, my wire child, an open tripod, and three cells:
The red room (the waiting room), a hat with cards, and a low angle view of treetops.
Stanley's *Paths of Glory* across from "can't get enough of that wonderful Duff"—et une
selection d'avoriaz 87.
Lisa stares out from a Dali parody,
The 60 greatest radio shows of the 20th Century and *AMPHIGOREY*
And now for something completely different . . .
Edited by Chris Rodley
A multi-colored beanie,
A picture book: *The Graveyards of Chicago*
Piano keys in black and white

—John, grade 12

Definition Poems

Another simple list poem is the definition poem. I ask students to choose a word that interests them and write a list of meanings for it. The list can take the shape of a dictionary definition, but it should not merely be a catalog of synonyms. The list should be specific and personal ("not what the dictionary says, but what it really should say," one student clarified). Here are two sample poems:

Tragedy: n., What my sister considers a broken nail or a paper cut; When my brother loses his ratty stuffed bald eagle named Bissy Boo when we're about to leave on a road trip; My brother when he announces that he has to use the bathroom when we're in the middle of Indiana; When the power goes out and

I'm in the middle of writing an important e-mail to my best friend; When I lose my diary at my nosy cousin Darya's house.

—Jessica grade 7

Beauty: (BYU-te) n., 1. The Blue Danube Waltz, 2. The book *2001: A Space Odyssey* signed by Arthur C. Clarke, 3. Infinite money and no parents around to tell me how to spend it, 4. Albert Einstein's Theory of Relativity in plain English, 5. Fermat's last theorem, 6. A clear view of night sky and an astronomy book full of constellations.

—Jeff, grade 6

It is important for students to feel good about their early work if they are to continue to take chances in their writing. This is particularly true because they usually come in with so many preconceptions about the abstruseness of poetry and an enormous lack of self-confidence. Through these early lessons, students learn to have fun with language and to work well together. I also want them to realize that poetry lives in specificity and that their individual perceptions are important for that reason: they can see and hear and feel and know things no one else can.

3 Same Pond, New Splash: Writing Modern English Haiku

the old pond—
a frog jumps in,
sound of water

    —Bashō

the smell of iron
as I come down the stairs—
winter evening

    —Lee Gurga

starry night
biting into a melon
full of seeds

    —Yu Chang

first snow
turning out the light
to see

    —Lidia Rozmus

winter sun begins
to warm the steering wheel—
prison visit day

    —Lee Gurga

Poems—even tiny poems—can offer powerful bursts of insight into our selves and the world around us. I move to haiku next because they are short and because they grow out of concrete perceptions of our everyday experiences.

In contrast to the formulaic 5-7-5 syllable form that many people think all haiku conform to, haiku poems remind us to rely on our own senses, our own perceptions, and to live more fully in the present moment. In the words of poet Gary Snyder, haiku help us "live where we are now." I begin teaching this verse form by writing on the board the five haiku that open this chapter. Rather than prescribing a set of rules, I ask students to infer the nature of haiku from these samples. Students are always good at identifying the general features of haiku: its brevity, the haiku "moment," the concrete images, and the juxtaposition of those images. In this chapter, I briefly explain these features and then present a sequence of writing exercises that culminates in students writing their own haiku.

Features of Haiku

Short Poems

Haiku are *typically* written as three short lines; they generally employ a *maximum* of seventeen syllables. Many fine haiku, however, have been written in two lines:

> withered corn rows
> the river in autumn
>
>   —Charles Trumbull

Or even in one:

> trying the old pump a mouse pours out
>
>   —Lee Gurga

Natural/Seasonal References

Haiku relate the natural world concretely—as it is, without the adornment of figurative language (such as simile, metaphor, and personification). Some students may wonder where the reference to nature is in the "smell of iron" poem. As human beings, we are part of nature, and, I believe, if haiku are to be useful in our daily lives, "nature" must include "human nature" as well. This is why haiku, like all poetry, can help us understand the world around us, ourselves, and our place in the world more fully.

Haiku Moment

Haiku grow from moments of epiphany, discoveries about the world and our place in it: a sunset, a leaf, the onset of winter, silence. Because haiku attempt to relate the poet's moment of heightened awareness of the world around him or her, haiku are generally written in the present tense (e.g., "winter sun begins to warm"); many haiku are deliberately written as sentence fragments (e.g., "first snow / turning out the light / to see"). This principle also explains the high premium haiku poets place on economy of language—a minimal presentation to imitate the immediacy of the moment.

Specific Images

Haiku are not abstract; they seek to capture the world as it is—concretely, vividly, immediately. As with all good descriptive writing, haiku find imagery in the five senses (the five model poems that open this chapter represent each of the five senses).

Juxtaposition of Images/Internal Comparison

Almost always in haiku there are two images, one on each side of a break, or caesura, in the poem. Without stating it explicitly, the "starry night" poem beautifully draws a parallel between a melon full of seeds and a night sky replete with stars.

In the rest of this chapter, I offer a series of short exercises that focus on these ingredients of modern haiku, culminating with students writing their own original haiku.

Writing Haiku

Word Seasons

One fun prewriting activity (also a nice minilesson on connotation) is to ask students to assign a corresponding season to a list of words. (Japanese poets might refer to a *kiyose,* a dictionary-sized catalog of seasonal references. The closest English equivalent is a recent attempt by American haiku poet William Higginson, whose *Haiku World* offers seasonal correspondences for hundreds of English words.) I start with some easy words: *icicle, suntan lotion, buds, fallen leaves;* some more ambiguous: *leaves, cherry trees, beach, tennis, shovel, moon;* some indeterminate: *telephone, kiss, ring, fire.* I ask students what personal experiences led them to the associations they make; these "stories" can become the basis for wonderful poems.

Asking students to justify the seasonal association they ascribe to each word leads to interesting debates, and students begin to imbue words with personal experience. When I asked one girl what season she associated with *handshake,* she said, "Definitely winter, since my grandmother died and I held her hand in the hospital." An eighth-grade boy said a handshake was "like spring" because he had just met a girl and the relationship was just beginning. Whatever the association, imagery in haiku, as in other genres, must carry a meaning that the reader can come to share.

Two-Word Poems

Teacher and poet Joseph Tsujimoto created another wonderful warm-up activity called the "two-word poem." In this exercise, students find two concrete nouns that resonate when put together. He offers these samples (41, 39, 38):

Scarecrow   Crucifix   Cathedral
  —Brady Onishi (grade 8)   Cascade
                                          —Fritz Johnson (grade 8)

Hands
                          birds
                          —Mary Caroline Richards

We think about the "stories" these pairs of words generate, noting that the most interesting combinations can elicit many different responses. We also discuss the order of the words, and how switching the words might create a very different poem. My students have always been fascinated by the way the top noun often takes on the modifying qualities of an adjective. The presentation of the words—especially Richards's pairing—can also greatly affect a poem's meaning.

My students created these:

nervous   grandfather
Jell-o   dollhouse

  —Mike, grade 8   —Claire, grade 8

mirror   glass
candy   veil

  — Arielle, grade 9   —Julie, grade 12

These two-word poems often make great titles. In fact, many works of art carry titles that would make lovely two-word poems: for example, the Paul Klee painting "Fish Magic"; The Beatles album *Rubber Soul*; the Jim Jarmusch film *Ghost Dog*; Louise Erdrich's novel *Love Medicine*. We return to two-word poems when we seek titles for our own collections (see Chapter 9).

Sandwich Poems

Next we write "sandwich poems," three-line poems in which the first two lines and the second two lines each form a different compound word. Here are a few examples:

crossing   recovering   fire
guard   alcoholic   alarm
rail   beverage   clock

These poems are not only fun to write, but they also help students understand resonance, the way in which an image can remain in the mind long enough to affect the next image in a poem. All of these activities focus on the specific and the concrete, and all feature single-word lines, in order to prepare students for difficult choices they will make in creating line breaks.

Cutting

Deciding where and how to create line breaks is one of the most challenging aspects of writing poetry. On the short canvas of a haiku, it is especially important to maximize the punch every end word carries. Traditional Japanese haiku poets took advantage of "cutting words," words that by their nature separate the two images in the haiku from each other. Without such a clearly defined set of words, modern English-language haiku poets need to create their own cutting words.

English-language haiku poets rely on a similar principle in creating line breaks in poems, taking advantage of the emphasis the last word in a line receives by ending lines with "strong" words—vivid nouns and verbs (rather than prepositions and articles that the reader cannot picture). This concept of understanding strong words will be useful in deciding where to make line breaks when students write different and longer kinds of poems later on.

Poets can also create divisions with punctuation such as dashes, periods, and colons, as in Bashō's "old pond" haiku. Haiku writing offers a great opportunity to teach the function rather than the form of punctuation marks (dashes: longer pauses; colons: movement from general to specific; semicolons: separating independent clauses and dividing balanced items of equal weight; commas: brief pauses; periods: rare, but full, long stops ending independent clauses). Some haiku (as in Yu Chang's "starry night") purposely feature no punctuation, taking advantage of the brief pause that line breaks afford and relating the poem as unfiltered experience to the reader. As reinforcement, I give students the following haiku without punctuation and ask them to insert appropriate marks:

his side of it.
her side of it.
winter silence

—Lee Gurga

in my medicine cabinet,
the winter fly
has died of old age.

—Jack Kerouac

awake!	not seeing
storm windows rattling	the room is white
in the nursery	until that red apple
—John S. O'Connor	—Anita Virgil

Together we compare their choices with the published models and discuss the efficacy of the choices.

Image Pools

When students are comfortable recognizing the form and function of haiku, they are ready to create original haiku of their own. As a final prewriting activity, I always give students a first line, have them create an image pool as a class, and then have them complete the poem by finding two lines from the image list on the board. Giving students a first line ensures a break in the poem and that a seasonal element will be considered. Last fall I gave my students this first line:

Halloween night—

Then I had them close their eyes and think about their most memorable Halloween night. Because images are created through the five senses, I asked students—whose eyes were still closed—to think of themselves in a particular place: What do you see—costumes, decorations, trees, cars, the sky? What do you hear—music? Screams? Children's voices? What do you smell—leaves? What do you taste—candy? What do you touch—a neighbor's hand? Candy wrappers? A bag or bucket? What costume did you wear?

Here is the list my students generated:

orange, electric lights, white face paint, Dracula, sunset, jack-o'-lanterns, brown paper bags, candy buckets, almost full moon, grabbing fingers, candy plates, warmth from open door, seeing your breath, haunted houses, warm clothes, parka, blue sky, crunchy leaves, shaving cream, All-saints, souls, El Dia de los Muertos, sinners, packs of kids, roaming, costumes (mummies, Little Mermaid, Tom and Jerry, Bugs Bunny, Michael Jordan, Darth Vader), good candy, stinky penny candy—Bazooka bubble gum—gangs, spears, pitchforks, flashlights, high-pitched trick-or-treat, howls, shouts, crinkly wrappers, laughter, "Monster Mash," chocolate kisses, smell of burned leaves, doors opened halfway, people blocking the view inside their homes, dark houses, watchful parents, school night, shadows.

A pretty impressive list, I think, and generated in just ten minutes. Here are two haiku we generated from this list:

Halloween night—
haunted house door
half-open

Halloween night—
the giant mouse
shadow

One student came up with this first draft:

Halloween night—
walking on leaves
near my house

This poem lacks the resonance of the first two because it is less specific. Haiku are so short there is no place for generality. This haiku needs to address the difficult "So what?" question. What does this poem reveal to the reader? What has the world revealed to the poet?

After writing this one on the board, I asked the class to offer the student suggestions for revision in the form of questions: Which of the five senses do the last two lines relate to? What was so special about the leaves? Why does it matter that it was your house? Were you barefoot?

The student ended up rewriting his haiku like this:

Halloween night—
the crunch of fallen
heart-shaped leaves

Now there's a haiku! It suggests a mood of ended love, or, given the opening line, perhaps that the end of the romance (or even the romance itself) is a sham, a game of make-believe. (The final two lines happen to form a line of iambic tetrameter, but I kept that to myself.)

There is a beautiful tradition in haiku of memorializing holidays in poems. For this reason, haiku make great classroom activities on holidays. Other "events" I have used include "first day of spring," "last day of school," "Halley's comet," and "first snow."

Reading haiku can suggest further topics and even supply new first lines for future poems. In Japan there is no shame whatsoever in borrowing a line from a poem you like; indeed, poets honor the earlier master by doing so. There, imitation truly is the sincerest form of flattery. Also, there is a firm belief among haiku poets that even a minor word change can transform a poem into something wholly original.

Poets can, of course, also pay tribute to the poem that inspired them by citing it below the new haiku.

Here are a few of my favorite student-written haiku:

full moon . . .
because my horoscope
said so

    —Colleen, grade 10

spring breeze—
the shrinking dot
that was a baseball

    —Grant, grade 12

in my backyard
a drop of water clings
to a dead orchid

    —Khoki, grade 9

college letter
my future does not fit
in an envelope

    —Grant, grade 12

train whistle blows
snow falls upward
from the tracks

    —Dan, grade 9

a homeless man
shivers
before a well-lighted place

    —Siqin, grade 12

speeding comet
still
in the night sky

    —Kiyoshi, grade 12

There is growing interest in haiku around the world, and many regional and several national and international haiku contests are open to school-age children every year. Haiku also has a wonderful social aspect. When I taught at University High, I started a club called U-High-ku in which students exchanged haiku with one another over lunch. (We even e-mailed poems to students in other states and other countries.) We also created a chapbook of our haiku poetry. (See the discussion of class books in Chapter 9.)

Reading and writing haiku make students more careful readers, better at understanding connotation and better at finding (and hearing) echoes in what they read. Teaching haiku also offers a wonderful opportunity to teach the importance of punctuation, line breaks, and sentence boundaries. In addition to these pedagogic advantages, haiku heightens students' awareness of themselves and their present environment. Oscar Wilde once said, "The great mystery of the world is not what is invisible, but what is visible." This notion is at the heart of haiku. Haiku helps students see better—what is around them and what is inside them, wherever they are.

4 Songs of Ourselves

I celebrate, and sing myself . . .
Walt Whitman, a kosmos, of Manhattan . . .
I am an acme of things accomplish'd, and I am an encloser of
things to be. . . .
Do I contradict myself? Very well then I contradict myself.
(I am large. I contain multitudes.)

> —Walt Whitman, from "Song of Myself"

These are excerpts from "Song of Myself," a dazzling list poem by Walt Whitman. Here the speaker sings of himself and searches for self-understanding, but Whitman's real subject is much larger. He celebrates all humankind and rejoices in the wonders of who we are, what we know, what we've experienced, and what we can become.

This limitless faith in the sheer potential of human beings is why I love Whitman's poetry and is, I suspect, why my students love his work as well. Young people, full of potential, feel limited, constrained by many forces: labels, expectations, stereotypes. Students rightly bristle at being reduced. Poetry helps us understand who we are and who we are not. Poetry invites us to examine how we see ourselves and how we are seen, and it allows us to define ourselves in ways other people might not. In the activities described in this chapter, students write poems about their names, abilities, knowledge, experiences, and potential.

Name Games

Ozymandias, Ishmael, Mudd, Scarlett O'Hara, Yogi Berra, Elmer Fudd. Names carry valuable information about who we are, where we come from, and what we hope others think of us. Names are also a safe, comfortable topic and one about which students are already somewhat expert. So what they don't know about their names can become the subject of a fun mini-research project.

Before assigning name poems, I like for students to meditate on their names. I want them to think about who they are and what they want to announce to the world. This is at the heart of all poetry. First, I pass out a copy of Sandra Cisneros's "My Name," a short chapter from her poetic novel *The House on Mango Street*, and some brief excerpts from Salman Rushdie's breathtakingly wordplayful novel *The Ground beneath Her Feet*:

In English my name means hope. In Spanish it means too many letters. It means sadness, it means waiting. It is like the number nine. A muddy color. It is the Mexican records my father plays on Sunday mornings when he is shaving, songs like sobbing.

It is my great-grandmother's name and now it is mine. She was a horse woman too, born like me in the Chinese year of the horse—which is supposed to be bad luck if you're born female—but I think this is a Chinese lie because the Chinese, like the Mexicans, don't like their women strong.

My great-grandmother. I would've liked to have known her, a wild horse of a woman, so wild she wouldn't marry. Until my great-grandfather threw a sack over her head and carried her off. Just like that, as if she were a fancy chandelier. That's the way he did it.

And the story goes she never forgave him. She looked out the window her whole life, the way so many women sit their sadness on an elbow. I wonder if she made the best with what she got or was she sorry because she couldn't be all the things she wanted to be. Esperanza. I have inherited her name, but I don't want to inherit her place by the window.

At school they say my name funny as if the syllables were made out of tin and hurt the roof of your mouth. But in Spanish my name is made out of a softer something, like silver, not quite as thick as sister's name—Magdelena—which is uglier than mine. Magdelena who at least can come home and become Nenny. But I am always Esperanza.

I would like to baptize myself under a new name, a name more like the real me, the one nobody sees. Especially as Lisandra or Maritza or Zeze the X. Yes. Something like Zeze the X will do. (Cisneros 10–11)

I began to use the workname "Rai" when I was taken on by the famous Nebuchadnezzar Agency. Pseudonyms, stage names, work names: for writers, for actors, for spies, these are useful masks, hiding or altering one's true identity, removing a disguise . . . since this had been Vina's private pet name for me—"Because you carry yourself like a little rajah," she'd told me. . . . That was Rai: a boy princeling. . . . It also meant desire: a man's personal inclination, the direction he chose to go in; and will, the force of a man's character. All that I liked. . . . And if on occasion I turned into "Hey, Ray" in that mighty democracy of mispronunciation, the United States, then I was not disposed to argue, [but] in another part of the world, Rai was music. . . . Most people don't even know my real name. Umeed Merchant, did I mention that? . . . The name Merchant, I should perhaps explain, means "merchant." Bombay families often bear names derived from some deceased ancestor's line of work. Engineers, Contractors, Doctors. And let's not forget the Readymoneys, the Cashondeliveris, the Fishwalas. And a Mistry is a mason, and a Wadia is a shipbuilder, and a lawyer is a Vakil and a banker is a Shroff. . . . Sodawaterbatilopenerwala, too. . . . Cross my heart and hope to die. Umeed, you see. Noun, feminine. Meaning hope." (Rushdie 18–19)

After students read these two passages, I have them write continuously for fifteen minutes, without lifting their pens off their papers, if possible. While they write, I pose the following list of questions:

1. What does your name mean?
2. Where does your name come from?
3. Who are you named after?
4. What is this person like? Do they look like you? Act like you?
5. Do you like or dislike being connected to this person by name? Why?
6. How did your parents settle on this name for you? Have you ever heard the story?
7. How about your middle name? (Repeat questions from above).
8. Do people ever call you by different names? Which do you prefer?
9. When do people call you by these different names?
10. What does your last name mean?
11. When people hear your name, what do they assume you'll look like? Sound like?
12. What nicknames do you go by? Which is your favorite? Why?
13. Who says your name closest to the way you say it? Who says it most beautifully? What does it sound like when this person says it? What does this person's mouth look like when he or she says your name?
14. Who says your name in the ugliest fashion? What does this person's mouth look like when he or she says your name?
15. How do people say your name when you've done something wrong?
16. How many letters are in your name? What else comes in sets of that same number?
17. What color does your name make you think of?
18. What substance is your name made out of? e.g., Gold, polyester, iron?
19. Have you ever given yourself a fake name? When? Why?
20. If you could rename yourself, which name would you choose and why?

After the final question, I give students an additional five minutes to continue writing or to look over what they've just written. Usually they are surprised at the length of their notes, and they are often surprised at the stories and characters (relatives, friends) they remember. When just a few students are still writing, I say, "Now find a good place to stop, and end with that line." I prefer to end freewriting gently rather than have students stop abruptly in midthought.

We then go around the room as I invite each person to read all or just a portion of what he or she has written. Most students are very interested in one another's stories, and they often look at their classmates in new ways when they hear of the various identities each person carries. This is also a great built-in revision exercise. As each person speaks, other students invariably say, "Oh, I forgot about my nicknames," or "I forgot to count the letters in my name." I assure them that they are always free to add details and stories later.

As students listen to one another's words, I ask them to pay attention to the most resonant, the most memorable, words and phrases. This is a good way to measure the class's understanding of specificity. After a few volunteers have read, I tell students to reread their own writing and underline the richest language. They should then choose some of these details as the material for a poem. They are free to expand details and scenes they began in the freewrite. Other than that, I don't impose any form on these poems. I want students to wrestle with the artistic problem of finding a form that suits their subject.

The following is a draft of a poem I wrote after a freewrite. I never really finished this piece, but I think it is important for students to see teachers struggling with the same artistic demands we ask them to tackle. Also, sharing personal writing—and this may be especially true with name poems—makes it easier for students to share their own writing with the teacher and with the class.

> My father worked construction,
> Wore a "uniform" of dark flannels
> So the dirt wouldn't show.
> He put up those green street lamps,
> With yellow domes of light
> Strong enough to read under,
> Though he never learned to read.
> My father left school when he was eight
> (His father died and he needed to work).
> He dug peat in the bogs, ten hours a day.

"John" sounds like bog, a one-syllable,
Dull thud of a name, like a black key
On a piano, worn thin over time.

My older brother was "John"
For three days until my father
Changed the birth certificate.
Now he's Mike for my father
And for my father's father.
I was named for my mother's father,
A man I never met.

John: four letters, four parts to Ireland,
Four angels answered my nighttime prayers:
One at the head, two at the feet,
And one to guard me while I'd sleep.

Once, in French class,
We had the chance
To take a new name.
I chose Napoleon—
The conqueror, not the creampuff.
"Now there's a man," I thought,
"Who really knew his history."

In turning a huge pool of words into a short coherent poem, I've found the speaker's attitude to be particularly important. One girl named Lea said she "was stuck" until she arrived at this opening:

"I am not your pretty little meadow.
I don't care for bunnies or wildflowers.
I am strong, like iron . . ."

Here is another student's freewrite:

Wisdom in both Korean and American. No, in America it's just some strange jumble of letters no one can pronounce. That's why I'm Sophia in America and Jihe in Korea. I'm not named after anyone. Koreans make up names for newborns. They, my parents, took the first character in my name from my Mom and combined it with another character to get my name. My name is very popular in Korea. Not in America. They can't even say it here. Only Koreans can say it properly. I'll answer to both names though. Sophia or Jihe. Or Soaps, Soapie. I hate sofa, though. I don't know

how Rachel even came up with that. She can't do anything to my
Korean name, though. <u>I actually don't like my name Sophia that
much. Too worldly and intelligent sounding. I wish it were
simple. 2 syllables, like my Korean name.</u>

The underlined words refer to the passages the student decided were
the most resonant. From this rich material, she crafted this poem:

Wisdom

My name, Jihe, means wisdom in Korea,
But not in America.
People can't even pronounce my name here.
It becomes a strange gibberish,
Maybe Russian? Maybe German?
Meaning nothing.

My other name, Sophia,
Also means wisdom,
But in Greek.
I suppose that's why
My parents decided to use it
For my Baptism.

Where do I come from?
No one country.
I come from wisdom,
Nowhere else.

—Sophia, grade 10

And here's a poem written by a first-year student, following the same
steps:

Name

It was an argument; was I to be Viola or Lilla?
Viola, my father said, sounded like an instrument.
So, Lilla I became, Lilla after Ella Lillian, my great grandmother,
A "great lady" with a taste for earrings.
People say it for the first time with delight, usually Italians
Bubbling the word, like sweet champagne.
Americans mangle it into "Lila" which sounds like
Dead cats, and wet plastic, and cheap perfume.
When they're sick of me,

My parents spit it at me, like a broken fingernail, and I hate it.
But, Lilla, whispered to yourself?
I think of
Perhaps pink peppercorns and a bit of brown sugar.
No name suits me better,
But with a second chance, I'd call me
Ella

—Lilla, grade 9

I Contain Multitudes

We are, of course, more than our names. One of the most interesting points of discussion that inevitably grows out of the name poems is how names can be great sources of pride and yet how names can limit. People are judged by gender, by age, by their relatives, by their ethnicity, and so forth. Most students are good at generating this list. Poetry, however, offers an antidote: the refusal to be limited. Whitman's "Song of Myself" is such a poem, as is Nikki Giovanni's "I Am She":

I Am She

I am she . . . making rainbows . . . in coffee cups . . . watching fish jump . . . after midnight . . . , in my dreams . . .

On the stove . . . left front burner . . . is the stew . . . already chewed . . . certain to burn . . . as I dream . . . of waves . . . of nothingness . . .

Floating to shore . . . riding a low moon . . . on a slow cloud . . . I am she . . . who writes . . . the poems . . .

—Nikki Giovanni

After students read sections of Whitman's poem and Nikki Giovanni's "I Am She," I ask them to write their own "song of myself" poem. Students never find this writing assignment daunting, because these poems are simply slightly longer list poems of the kind discussed in Chapter 2. Many students, however, tell me they are not often called upon to announce their powers, their gifts—neither the ones people know about nor the ones that have gone undiscovered. I like the invitation to celebrate ourselves that this assignment provides. I challenge students to go beyond the obvious and immediate sensations, and to feel free to refute the false notions people have of them.

One of the best outcomes of this assignment is the attitude the poem invites students to take. Here are some examples:

I Am

I am a tuna swimming in the fish-filled coral.
I am an ivory bracelet hugging your wrist.
I am a bicep, always growing stronger.
I am J.C. Penny's with people always swarming in and out like
  bees.
I am a post card being sent to Italy.
I am the William H. Ray School, lonely with kids out for the
  summer.
I am a comb running through your dark, silky hair.
I am a cherry colored sports car just filled with gas.
I am a tuna, swimming along the fish-filled coral . . . with many
  destinations to go.

—Zarinah, grade 7

Who Am I?

Am I
White: German, French, Dutch?
Native American: Cherokee, Navajo?
Black: African, West Indian?
        NO
I am not a Caucasian;
My skin is too dark,
My hair too coarse.
I am not an American Indian:
I do not ride horses bareback,
And I do not sleep in a teepee.
I am not African-American.
My skin is too light,
My hair too fine.
        NO
They call me
Mulatto, mutt, mixed,
Half-breed, black, colored.

They ask:
Are you Puerto Rican, chica?
Are you Asian?
Italian?

Is that your real hair?
Are those your real eyes?
What exactly are you?

I am not under your control
Because of whatever my race might be.
You can't fit me into a box
'Cuz I know who I am . . .
I'm ME!

—Nicki, grade 10

Many students write poems of surprising power with simple list prompts such as these. I've also asked students to write lists of "Lies I've told/been told"; "Promises I've kept/broken" (especially after they've read W. C. Williams's "This Is Just to Say"); and, from Kenneth Koch's book *Wishes, Lies and Dreams:* "I Used to Be _____, but now I am _____." One student, writing about his transition from elementary school, wrote, "I used to be Captain America, but now I'm just another middle schooler." Sometimes these exercises become finished poems, sometimes not. But they are almost always useful for mining our experiences for rich material to use in later pieces.

Here are some excerpts from a class of ninth graders:

I used to be a baby, but now I am a bigger baby.
I used to be carefree, but now I care.
I used to know everything, now I know nothing.
I used to make paper dolls but now I just make papers.
I used to be small, but now I am smaller.
I used to be the baby of the family, now I'm the baby-sitter of
    the family.

I used to be a fisherman, now I'm just a fish.
I used to be a little girl, but now I am an old woman.
I used to be afraid of ghosts, but now I'm afraid of people.
I used to trust everything, but now I am aware.
I used to check for monsters under the bed, now I check the
    news.
I used to be a fairy princess in a tall, gray brick castle, but now
    I am a freshman in high school.

I used to want to become a clown, but now I want to become a
    cardiologist.
I used to chatter when we went hiking, but now my steps are
    silent on the stones.

I used to write angry poems in my diary, but now I just describe the day.
I used to want to grow up, but now I'm holding on to my youth.
I used to read books of poetry, but now I'm composing my own.

I used to be pretty, but now I'm elevationally impaired.
I used to be a rock star, but now my hair is just purple, and green, and pink.
I used to have a brother, but now I have a leather jacket.
I used to hate going to church, but now I see the point.
I used to stare blankly at saints' stony faces, but now I just sleep in on Sundays.

I used to sleep with a light on, but now I sleep better when all is dark.
I used to be afraid of confrontation, but now I like to stir it up.
I used to be able to fit in my teddy bear clothes, but now I can't get them over my head.
I used to rule my own kingdom, but now I can't even vote.
I used to wonder how babies were born, but now I wished I had never asked.
I used to be afraid of wind, but now I just close the window.
I used to be magically invisible, but now I'm just ignored.

These list poems allow great variability as long as the subject matter—how students see themselves and how they see their former and future selves—remains important. Here are a few lines from the same class of ninth graders responding to a different prompt: I am (a) _____, but (one day) I'll be (a) _____:

I'm short right now, but one day I'll be beautiful.

I'm a child, but one day I'll meet my grandchildren.

I'm half-black now, but one day I'll just be human.

I'm a human being, but one day I'll be an angel.

I'm tough, but I'll learn how to be sympathetic.

I am perfect, but one day I will shatter.

I'm fatherless, but one day I'll be a father.

I'm shy, but one day I'll say everything on my mind.

I know "right and wrong," but one day I'll act right.

I'm loved, but one day I'll miss being missed.

I am a C student, but one day I'll be a woman.

I am a bacteria, but one day I hope to be a mold.

I am putting the baby dolls in storage, but one day I'll bring them out again.

I am a feather, but one day I'll be a pillow.

Right now I speak with words, but one day I'll speak with actions.

I'm safe for now, but one day I'll be in danger.

These list poems are rare entrées into students' hopes and dreams and allow students to reflect on ideas that are bubbling powerfully within them but that rarely come to the surface of their consciousness. I am astonished at the ways in which students see themselves, their future world, and their future selves. Some lines also offer fascinating glimpses into students' personal notions of happiness and success.

Similar prompts work equally well. After reading Langston Hughes's "The Negro Speaks of Rivers," for example, one student wrote this poem:

Places

I would like to visit Alaska and dog sled across the barren, icy tundra.
I would like to visit Hawaii and gaze at a monstrous, black volcano on a Martian landscape.
I would like to visit Australia and swim in the vast blue reefs with beautiful fish.
I would like to visit Italy and eat spaghetti till it comes out my ears.
I would like to visit Switzerland and ski, ski, ski on the beckoning Alps.

—Jessica, grade 7

"I, too, am untranslatable," Walt Whitman writes in "Song of Myself"—and not just to other people. We are often "untranslatable" even to ourselves. Poems—even relatively simple list poems—can help us see who we are, who we were, and who we can be in the boundless worlds of our imagination.

5 Presences and Absences

Inside this pencil
crouch words that have never been written
never been spoken
never been taught

they're hiding

they're awake in there
dark in the dark
hearing us . . .

    —W. S. Merwin, from "The Unwritten"

Another way we express our identity is through our relations to the world around us. In the preceding poem, W. S. Merwin's speaker suggests that the ordinary objects in our lives, such as common pencils, are full of interesting stories about who we are, and that these stories from the tangible world can help us understand the intangible. In particular, our relationship to the physical world can reveal profound truths about our values, emotions, ideas, and attitudes.

In this chapter, I present activities that help students explore the presences and absences in their environments: what they are surrounded by, what they choose to surround themselves with, and what happens when our relationship to our surroundings changes. Students have already explored part of their world, writing the map poems discussed in Chapter 2, and later they will explore the personalities of their hometowns and neighborhoods (see Chapter 7). But here our focus is smaller. "All truths wait in things," Walt Whitman said, so I ask students to focus on the concrete objects in their lives—what we have and what we have lost.

Object Lessons

One year, while studying Lillian Hellman's *The Little Foxes*, a class of eighth graders was struck by the objects in Horace Giddens's safety deposit box: his daughter's baby shoe, a cheap cameo on a string, and a piece of an old violin. We talked about how objects sometimes take on a great emotional significance far surpassing their material value.

I told my students a story about my childhood. When I was four years old, my family lived in a huge apartment building on the west side of Chicago. The entire complex went up in smoke one night. I never learned the cause of the fire, but I do remember standing on the curb across the street. My entire family held hands like a paper chain family, staring in disbelief at the fire. We lost nearly everything: most of our family photos, clothes, toys. I remember how attached I became to the few remaining objects. I especially remember a new pair of moccasins I was wearing outside. (For years I imagined I was Native American and visited the Indian rooms of the Natural History Museum with inextinguishable interest.) I also remember my stuffed animal, a large golden dog named Cuddly Duddly. I carried that dog with me for years, never minding how filthy and ragged he had become.

I wanted students to think about their possessions and why we invest some of these possessions with so much meaning. Few people I know take the time to ask such questions of themselves. Speaking of the objects that make up his world, Octavio Paz writes somewhere that "they live alongside us. We do not know them. They do not know us. But sometimes they speak with us." I decided to take his words literally, asking students to gather their most prized possessions and to let the objects "speak" about what their owners value, what matters most deeply to them.

When I asked students to name their most prized possessions, objects to which they attached the most significance, their response overwhelmed me. In addition to writing about the objects, students asked if they could bring the objects into class. I agreed, of course, and we had a show-and-tell day that was one of our most meaningful classes.

In *Art as Experience,* John Dewey commented that works of art are too often set apart from "the scope of common or community life" (6). Here, by using the actual materials of our lives to craft poems, students saw that their possessions—even ordinary objects of little market value—carried enormously rich artistic value: the value of their experiences. The class came together as a community, reverentially listening to one another's stories and, where appropriate, passing the objects around the room as if they were sacred icons.

I asked students to choose one or more of their most cherished possessions and write from the object's point of view, to give the object a voice. Some students called this exercise a "safety deposit box poem"— after the scene in *The Little Foxes* mentioned earlier—since the resulting poems are derived from objects they secretly treasure. Here are two untitled examples:

> I am two porcelain cats
> Parts broken,
> Isolated from the rest of my family,

Yet full of life.
One is striped, one spotted
The smallest of our kind,
Yet most powerful, more important
Than all the rest.

                          —Weiwei, grade 8

I am an old baseball glove, worn and old,
    but still catching all the scorching grounders and floating flies.
I am an army of packed knights, clustered, jumbled,
    huddled together, traveling, wandering, fighting to keep hold.
I am a set of ear tubes, pink like a pig,
    stopping the squealing pain.
I am a set of chisels: sad and rusty,
    sitting alone, dying in pain.

                          —Drew, grade 8

Odes to Common Things

We rarely publicly proclaim or praise the people, places, and things that enrich our lives. This is a shame since, according to W. H. Auden, "There is only one thing poetry must do: it must praise all it can for being and happening"(qtd. in Hirsch 80). I ask my students to write songs of praise about their worlds through odes.

Odes are usually dedicated to monumental heroes or lofty ideas. Pablo Neruda, however, revolutionized the form in three books of odes to mundane subjects. In *Odes to Common Things*, for example, he writes poems to his dog, to french fries, to his socks. In the opening poem, "Ode to Things," he says that things "were / so close / [to me] that they were a part / of my being, / they were so alive with me / that they lived half my life / and will die half my death."

I ask students to think of features of their worlds that are most special to them, encouraging them to pick one-of-a-kind objects, but any topic will do. (The former poet laureate Robert Pinsky wrote an ode to television in the book *Jersey Rain*.) I do, however, ask my students to concentrate on things rather than abstract terms such as *love* or *peace*, because objects usually lead to more concrete description. Students praise all the virtues of this object, telling the world why this object is so marvelous and why the poet holds the object in such a special relation. I pass out a few of Neruda's poems as models. Here is an excerpt from "Ode to My Socks":

Two socks as soft
as rabbit fur.
I thrust my feet
inside them
as if they were
two
little boxes
knit
from threads
of sunset
and sheepskin.
My feet were
two woolen
fish
in those outrageous socks,
two gangly,
navy-blue sharks
impaled
on a golden thread,
two giant blackbirds,
two cannons:
thus
were my feet
honored
by
those
heavenly
socks.
They were so beautiful
I found my feet
unlovable
for the very first time,
like two crusty old
firemen, firemen
unworthy
of that embroidered
fire,
those incandescent socks.

     —Pablo Neruda

Here are a few sample poems my students have written in response:

Lunchtime

O, brown paper lunch bags,
Beneath my fingers
You produce a melody
Of crunching sounds,
Or, when filled with air,
A harmonious boom.

Your thin paper is the perfect surface
For writing
The name of your owner,
A phone number,
A quick note,
A poem,
Or even a game of tic-tac-toe.

You give the appearance
Of being plain,
Ordinary,
Boring—
A clear misconception

So easily can you become
                    a paper airplane,
                    a fortune teller,
                    a sailboat,
                    or a puppet.
                    You can even catch my hiccups,

                    And best of all,
                    at lunch time
                    when my stomach growls
                    the glorious vision of you
                    reassures me.

                                   —Maya, grade 10

Ode to Coffee

O, glorious coffee,
How I love to hear the gurgle of the bubbling brew
As it fills my steaming coffee pot.

Your smooth liquid slips down my esophagus
With serpentine ease.
Your sweet taste lingers on dancing tastebuds.
And, your temple? Your holy house?
It proclaims itself in green and white,
And the whole world seems pathetic in its light.
Starbucks:
With its cappucinos and frappucinos,
Mochas and lattes
(where small is tall).
None shall ever compare to you.
You are the first,
The only,
The true.

—Danielle, grade 10

I like the variety of possibilities odes offer as these writers explore the connections between their identity and the environments that surround them. The coffee poem delivers a humorous panegyric to an ordinary—but vital!—part of life for many of us. The speaker in the paper bag poem may be suggesting that she is taken for granted or overlooked when she clearly seems to be full of surprises, imagination, and good humor.

One student took the assignment in a surprising way, writing this touching poem:

Ode to the Hyde Park Crazy Guy

O, Crazy Guy!
Always there by the lake
With your trusty umbrella
Rain or shine.
Singing your nonsensical songs
Spouting obscenities
At innocent
Passers-by.

Who knows why you are always there?
Who knows why you carry that umbrella?

All I know
Is that when I run down by the lake
In the afternoon

And you are not there
To throw rocks as I pass
My life feels empty.

—Robyn, grade 10

This poet describes a locally well-known "crazy" man (actually, he is an erstwhile brilliant biologist who was stricken with schizophrenia) in extraordinarily compassionate terms. Whereas many people might shut this man out of their minds the way one might ignore a lamppost, this speaker recognizes this man's humanity—even if as a disturbing presence—as part of her world.

Loss Poems

Losses offer another measure of who we are. Whether for the better (weight, fear of flying) or for the worse (a favorite pen, a pet, a loved one), losses help define us—who we were before the loss and who we are right now. Taking a cue from Naomi Shihab Nye's wonderful anthology titled *What Have You Lost?*, I sometimes ask students to write lists of things they've lost, ranging from the trivial to the immense. Here is one student's response:

I Have Lost

The First Harry Potter Book.
My interest in the book *Tangerine*.
My science homework.
Three single dollars in one load of wash.

I have lost
Two soccer balls: one Nike, one Wilson.
A pair of Nike running shoes.
A pair of socks—that were once white.
Penn Tennis balls.
The hope of ever winning a soccer game.
A Bulls T-shirt.
A Cubs baseball cap.

I have lost
My own hair
A wig.
A toupee (not mine).

I have lost
A toy bulldozer.
A toy turkey,
A set of 500 matchbox cars and trucks.
A green Gameboy Pocket.
Countless computer games.

I have lost
Friends that moved away.
My dog Lucky.
And lastly my five fish: Fred, Fred, Fred, Fred
And Speedy.

—BJ, grade 7

This writer juxtaposes interesting words and groups similar terms; he is beginning to think about stanzas. He also hears the power of repetition: the title line that opens each stanza. Particularly with these early assignments, I want students to abandon their preconceptions about poems. Everyday items are fine subjects for poems. Poems can be funny or serious. They don't need to rhyme. I remind them: poems live in specificity and delight us with surprising sounds and ideas.

Another student defines her losses within a specific year:

Things I Lost in Fourth Grade

A praying mantis
A roll of scotch tape
A fake nail

A green silk sock
An opal earring
A friend

A burgundy sweater
A silver button
My grandmother

A tube of lavender lip gloss
A plastic spider monkey
A year

—Tara, grade 9

I like the way this poet describes specific objects with concrete details. The three-line stanzas also lend the poem great shape and power, particularly since the final lines of each stanza read as blunt punctuations to the preceding lines.

I often have students write about an individual loss from their lists, especially if I think the description of the loss reveals a strong emotion behind it. Here is a poem taken from Nye's *What Have You Lost?:*

My Father's Coat

My father's coat was made
of the finest muscle. Fish-scales
were its lining;
from them, waterfalls
glistened. Rainbow trout
swam in the depths of its pockets
among twigs and polished stones.
Inside this coat, my father
was invisible. He became
the smell of wet leaves,
the smoke of campfires,
and when he wrapped me in his
sleeves, I stepped inside
the dark forest.

—Suzi Mee

Here a common item sparks a rich imaginative world, complete with flora and fauna. I am always amazed at how much of ourselves is invested in and comes to be represented by ordinary objects.

One student ended her list of losses with this line: "my grandfather, three years ago." She said she was interested in writing more about this man she loved, but found his loss difficult to write about until she found an object that allowed her to begin to express her deep affection and deep sense of loss. Here is her final poem:

Ziggy

Blue-white Manischewitz-Jahrzeit candle
In its glowing glass jar
Bought on sale at the Co-op, two for 89 cents
Three in the medicine closet means
Three more years to remember

Remember September 22nd?
A rushed Sunday morning

Go back to sleep
Tuesday funeral
No school for me
Drizzling rain and black umbrellas

Beta videos of an old man
With wild Albert Einstein hair
A scratchy voice
And an odd sense of humor
"Do you need this button?"
And when my mother said yes,
He'd yank it off and say,
"Here you go."
And laugh.

—Lisa, grade 12

Like T. S. Eliot's Prufrock, who "measured out his life in coffee spoons," this student uses memorial candles as a measure of the depth of her loss. And, in the process of expressing the pain she feels at her grandfather's absence, she finds comfort in the memory of his clowning.

This chapter discusses activities through which we can further explore our identity by writing about our relationships to the world, especially the things we have and the things we've lost. Chapter 6 features poems about memory and how we preserve our sense of identity in the world around us.

6 Avenues to the Past

"Y ou take your material where you find it," writes Tim O'Brien, "which is your life, at the intersection of past and present" (34). Memories are an extraordinarily rich source of artistic material. What and how we choose to remember say a great deal about who we are. Furthermore, there is something wonderfully unique about our memories, and I share this with my students: "No one else in the world knows your memories, knows what you know, your experiences, your perceptions." This is why *their* literature, their poetry, is so valuable.

I Remember

The feel of clothes just out of a dryer, the smell of too much cologne, the sound of car tires on gravel, the feel of an itchy mitten, the taste of soup so hot you have to slurp it into your mouth. Every reader of these descriptions can recall specific, vivid episodes in his or her past. Sensory descriptions are powerful tools for unlocking memories. Since we do quite a few exercises to develop concrete sensory description, it's not surprising that many of my students' best poems grow out of their memories. It is exciting to watch students tap into the memories of their personal experiences, to make connections between apparently disparate elements in their lives—who they once were and who they see themselves as being at the present moment.

As a prelude to writing memory poems, I ask students to write their most powerful memories in a list: I remember _____. I remember _____. Although students have already written list poems (see Chapters 2, 4, and 5), before we begin these lists, and even while students write, I read excerpts from Joe Brainard's wonderfully idiosyncratic *I Remember*, a book-length list poem that follows this pattern throughout. Here are some lines from his book:

> I remember the only time I saw my mother cry. I was eating apricot pie.
>
> I remember how much I used to stutter.
>
> I remember how much in high school, I wanted to be handsome and popular.
>
> I remember stories about razor blades being hidden in apples at Halloween.

I remember *almost* sending away for body building courses many times.

I remember our grade school librarian Miss Peabody. At the beginning of each class we had to all say in unison "Good morning, Miss Peabody." Only instead we said "Good morning, Miss Pee-body." I guess she decided to ignore it since she never said anything about it. She was very tall and very thin and there was always a ribbon or scarf tied around her head from which bubbled lots of silver-gray curls.

I remember "free day" in gym and usually picking stilts.

I remember wax fingernails. Wax mustaches. Wax lips. And wax teeth.

I remember eating out alone in restaurants trying to look like I had a lot on my mind.

I remember the exact moment during Communion that was the hardest to keep from smiling. It was when you had to stick out your tongue and the minister laid the white wafer on it.

Many students need a model to follow or their lines will be too short to be interesting. As students write, I walk around, encouraging them to fill out lines fully like the Brainard models and praising fully developed lines. After listening to some of Brainard's lines, a student who had written simply "I remember my grandfather's weird clothes" wrote "I remember my grandfather's polka-dotted bow tie and those argyle knee socks which he pulled past his knees."

The first time I asked students to jot down a list of memories, I was astonished to find several students stuck, unable to jot down a single line. A trick, I've learned, is to give students a minimum number of lines to shoot for: say, the first ten memories they can recall. Somehow, stipulating a minimum number makes the writing task concrete and manageable for everyone. I have never had a student who couldn't reach the minimum number.

One student wrote this list he later entitled "Frozen Preserves":

I remember accidentally swallowing my gum when I walked into a forest preserve one morning with my father.

I remember the white mush spurting from a large bug after my grandfather whacked it with a bedroom slipper.

I remember an elderly woman looking like a wind-up toy, happily bobbing with her raised elbows moving back and forth and her feet taking short quick steps.

I remember trying to look funny in front of my best friend by eating my cereal with orange juice and almost vomiting.

I remember eating peanut butter pretzels in the dim yellow
light underneath an umbrella opened against the spitting
shower faucet in the guest bathroom.

I remember lying on my back and gazing directly into the
ceiling light without blinking until tears traveled over my ears
and darkened the hallway carpet.

I remember mistaking a dead pigeon for a glove before I
came close to it lying among the raised roots of a tree.

And I remember knowing after I tried to lift it that its stiff
wings were frozen to the snowy ground.

—John, grade 12

These lines are filled with rich, specific descriptions that only this
author could have written. He took great care ordering the lines and
finding links between apparently random memories: the initial movement from father to grandfather; the funny-looking elderly woman and
the speaker trying to act funny; the bathroom and hallway lights. It's
especially great that the final line offers a change of pace, opening with
the word *And*, which by itself suggests the close of the poem. The final
line not only relates to the preceding line (also about the pigeon), but it
also returns to the opening lines—the frozen preserve. This gives the
poem a circular unity, like the word association list poems (see Chapter
2).

These "I remember" lists are also easy to focus for specific pur-
poses. Students could, for example, write a memory list about a time
they were scared, a time they felt safe, a time they felt independent,
abandoned, accepted, and so on. Often these focused lists are complete
poems in themselves. Here is one such student list poem:

I remember Hurricane Andrew. I remember waking up to find
my grandmother was not in the bed beside me, and the light
we had left on the night before was off, indicating the power
was out. I was in Miami with my aunt and uncle. My little
cousin was three weeks old to the day. I remember huddling in
a small hallway, no more than six feet long and four feet wide. I
remember being scared and even excited. I could have died
that night. I remember the screams of the wind, almost human.
I could almost see a woman outside our door, screaming, but I
knew it was just the wind. I remember having to go to the
bathroom in front of everyone, since I was too scared to shut
the door, on a toilet that would not flush. I remember listening

to a battery-powered radio, hearing about people whose rooms and loved ones were torn away from them as they stood there, clinging to their very lives. We had taken all of the mangos off the tree the night before in case there was a hurricane, so they would not come hurtling toward the house. I remember waiting in the deadly silence of the eye of the storm for it to resume. It never did. I remember finding a phone and calling my parents to say I was okay.

—Lisa, grade 9

Incredibly, this beautiful list is a first draft. I love the fully developed sensory descriptions (the screams of the wind, the battery-powered radio, the mangos). This list also has a built-in structure: before (and during the nightmare storm) and after (the storm had subsided).

Students can also experiment with eliminating the "I remember" tag *after* they have finished their lists. Lloyd Schwartz's "Nostalgia (The Lake at Night)"—which reads like an "I remember" poem with the refrain erased—beautifully evokes a mood by listing the speaker's sensory impressions. I often ask students to close their eyes and imagine they are living in the setting of this poem as I read it slowly aloud:

The black water.

Lights dotting the entire perimeter.

Their shaky reflections.

The dark tree line.

The plap-plapping of water around the pier.

Creaking boats.

The creaking pier.

Voices in conversation, in discussion—two men, adults— serious inflections (the words themselves just out of reach).

A rusty screen-door spring, then the door swinging shut.

Footsteps on a porch, the scrape of a wooden chair.

Footsteps shuffling through sand, animated youthful voices (*how many?*)—distinct, disappearing.

A sudden guffaw, some giggles; a woman's—no, a young girl's—sarcastic reply; someone's assertion; a high-pitched male cackle.

Somewhere else a child laughing.

Bug-zappers.

Tires whirring along a pavement . . . not stopping . . . receding.

Shadows from passing headlights.

A cat's eyes caught in a headlight.

No moon.

Connect-the-dot constellations filling the black sky—the ladle of the Big Dipper not quite directly overhead.

The radio tower across the lake, signalling.

Muffled quacking near the shore; a frog belching; crickets, cicadas, katydids, etc.—their relentless sexual messages.

A sudden gust of wind.

Branches brushing against each other—pine, beech.

A fiberglass hull tapping against the dock.

A sudden chill.

The smell of smoke, woodstove fires.

A light going out.

A dog barking; then more barking from another part of the lake.

A burst of quiet laughter.

Someone in the distance calling someone too loud.

Steps on a creaking porch.

A screen-door spring, the door banging shut.

Another light going out (you must have just undressed for bed).

My bare feet on the splintery pier turning away from the water.

Here is one student's poem that greatly benefited from dropping the "I remember" tag:

lake

moon over
  that summer lake
  mini-golf by moonlight

no light by the telephone
a breeze so chilly I needed two sweatshirts
and shivered all the next day
hot water; hot tub
rowboat rocking in the wake of a jet-ski
rowboat drifting under dark gray thunderclouds
rain gushing down, past the porch screens
playing poker on the porch
porch to pier with flashlights
glimmer of the lake, barely visible at night

—Abigail, grade 12

This is a nice, spare poem; even the single-word, lowercase title reveals how wonderfully stripped down these evocative perceptions are. The verbs (*rocking, gushing, shivering*) are especially vivid, and I like the balance in line 7. She repeats some terms (*rowboat, porch*) and new details each time.

Memory Poems

After they've written their memory lists, I ask each student to star two related lines (two related memories) and to expand these lines into fuller descriptions. This is an especially good way to get students to think about stanzas. I encourage them to find surprising connections. Looking back at the Brainard list, there are clear connections between lines 5 and 7: they both deal with Brainard's flirtation with strength and physical power. Lines 4 and 8 might make an interesting little poem about Halloween.

One student helped me see a connection between this exercise and the two-word poems we had written earlier (see Chapter 2). Among the items in his list were the lines "I remember building an igloo out of snow and ice and wanting to live in it" and "I remember the time my parents told me they were getting a divorce." He read these descriptions as causally related: he wanted to build the igloo—a refuge from his icy-cold emotional life at home—in response to the distressing news of his parents' divorce. This, he rightly said, would make a great two-word poem:

divorce
igloo

Here is his finished poem:

Chapter 6

country ice

I remember the summers
in the country with my cousins.
We had mudfights with the mud
we dug off the bottom of the pond.

I remember an ice storm,
the frozen lake
beyond the bent and broken trees—
all alone
coated in ice.

I remember when I was small
I dreamed of a snowstorm,
snow up to my waist,
so I could build an igloo
that I could hide in.

—Peter, grade 11

The following poem drops the "I remember" tag, but it retains a key juxtaposition of images from the author's original list that results in a jolting ending:

Poppy

In chair 306,
Cubs park
Two seats left from Poppy,
my grandpa.
The hot green metallic chair against my back.
Red hot in my right hand.
Big Coke in the other.
Watching the players run the bases,
No thought in my head about death.

—Greg, grade 11

In every class, I am astonished by several memory poems, and students often surprise themselves by what they remember and how they remember important people, places, and ideas in their lives. Juxtaposing memories, even memories that seemed unrelated at first glance, can be magical, forcing us to reconsider each memory as new in light of the other.

Photograph Poems

Perhaps the most common way we physically store memories is through photographs. I started using photographs as poem prompts because they provide a concrete visual field for students to describe. I like the idea of students holding photos—meaningful possessions from their own lives—as their subjects. Before we begin writing, we look at models such as Sharon Olds's "Photograph of the Girl" and Raymond Carver's "Photograph of My Father in his Twenty-Second Year."

Photograph of the Girl

The girl sits on the hard ground,
the dry pan of Russia, in the drought
of 1921, stunned,
eyes closed, mouth open,
raw hot wind blowing
sand in her face. Hunger and puberty are
taking her together. She leans on a sack,
layers of clothes fluttering in the heat,
the new radius of her arm curved.
She cannot be not beautiful, but she is
starving. Each day she grows thinner, and her bones
grow longer, porous. The caption says
she is going to starve to death that winter
with millions of others. Deep in her body
the ovaries let out her first eggs,
golden as drops of grain.

—Sharon Olds

The subject of this poem—"the girl"—is undetermined, so it is not clear what relation the speaker has to her. It could be anyone, a family member or a total stranger. Our clearest clue comes late in the poem when the speaker uses the word *caption,* making it seem now as if the speaker is looking through a history book. The final image of "her first eggs" like "drops of grain" is unbearably sad. This reminds us how young the girl is, and it returns to the earlier description of the barren land that will result in widespread starvation.

Photograph of My Father in His Twenty-Second Year

October. Here in this dank, unfamiliar kitchen
I study my father's embarrassed young man's face.

Sheepish grin, he holds in one hand a string
of spiny yellow perch, in the other
a bottle of Carlsbad beer.

In jeans and denim shirt, he leans
against the front fender of a 1934 Ford.
He would like to pose bluff and hearty for his posterity,
Wear his old hat cocked over his ear.
All his life my father wanted to be bold.

But the eyes give him away, and the hands
that limply offer the string of dead perch
and the bottle of beer. Father, I love you,
yet how can I say thank you, I who can't hold my liquor either
and don't even know the places to fish?

—Raymond Carver

Most of this poem is a careful description of the speaker's father that uses beautiful, specific details (his grin, the beer, the fish, the hat). But the speaker opens the poem with the announcement that he is a character here, too, studying his father's photograph. I love the tension and the dialogue this movement creates. It prepares us for the direct address in the third stanza ("Father, I love you"). He seems to have lost his father and now is speaking to him the only way he can, through the memory channel of a photograph. The speaker seems to be asking for guidance of some sort, which makes us reevaluate the beginning word *October*. His father is a young man in the picture, yet the speaker (or at least his mood) seems autumnal.

Writing Photograph Poems

Almost everyone collects some photographs as records of their lives. Each year in school "Picture Day" is a source of excitement or anxiety for many students. Our emotional investment in photographs is enormous: How do people look? How do we want them to look? What have we chosen to record? How has it been preserved? What has gone undocumented?

Apart from their emotional content, photographs are wonderful writing tools because they are so concrete; you can hold them in your hands. I also like the way students respond to one another's photos—with fascination and respect and even awe (with older photographs), just as they did with their prized possessions (see Chapter 5).

When I simply asked students to "carefully describe a photo that carries special meaning to you, describing everything in the frame," they did a very nice job of relating the visual contents of the photograph, but these descriptions became poems, I think, when I added an element of tension to the assignment: "Write about what is not in the frame: the photographer, missing signs of the setting, the occasion, an important person who is not pictured. Your poem should reconcile/explain why the contents of the frame do not contain all the information necessary to understand the event fully."

Sometimes students tell me they took the pictures themselves or that they remember the event precisely. If not, I encourage them to ask their family and friends for additional information. In either case, students create rough drafts by listing the contents of the photograph and then a separate list of items or ideas not pictured. Then I tell them to find ways in which the second list connects with the first, the way they did in searching through their "I remember" lists. This assignment almost always yields wonderful poems. Here are a few student samples:

Holiday

Even on holidays
We're not
All together.
My dad and I sit in a BIG red armchair
He looking dead
At the camera;
I look down
At my new Minnie Mouse slippers.
My father puts the slippers on my feet,
He holds me,
Calls me his
Little girl.
I am safe
In my daddy's arms.

My fake mother is taking the picture.
My real Mom sits at her house
All alone.
Another X-mas divided by the two
Of you.

—Ashleigh, grade 10

This poem is both very sad and very beautiful. The line breaks (especially after *not, dead,* and *down*) are devastating. "They" are not a "we." To the speaker, her father is dead in a way now that he is divorced. The speaker is downcast in addition to looking at her feet. Many students turn this assignment into a two-stanza poem: what's in the picture and what's not. But they don't have to write their poems in this manner. Here, in addition to the stanza break, there is a jump in diction. The word *fake* jumps out at the reader, as does the capitalization of the "real" Mom. Actually there are several divisions in this poem: the two houses; the photographer from her subjects; the speaker's current and former views of her father.

Verdun, France, April, 1915

Playful and proud
You glance away from your airplane
Oblivious to the pilot
Who explains its controls.
That "modern" machine with bicycle tires,
A wooden propeller,
Paper-thin wings that will carry you,
Co-pilot,
Thousands of feet into the air
To shoot pictures across enemy lines.
A couple yards away
Your buddies are sitting around casually
Smoking hand-rolled cigarettes
And gawking playfully at your girlfriend
Whose hands shake so much that she can hardly
Take the photograph.

—Sylvain, grade 11

This poem opens with a nice alliterative line and uses specific details throughout (the hand images at the end, for example). That the phrase "co-pilot" gets its own line is interesting because the speaker's subject, his grandfather, is a co-pilot in perhaps two senses—an Air Force pilot and a young man about to marry the woman who is taking his picture.

Moon Beyond

I can see the muscle in his weak arm
As he carries the empty milk jug.

He has helped his wife milk the cows,
Without smiling or laughing.
A frown always on his face,
A hat always on his head.

He never said "Bonjour,"
Or acknowledged my presence.
He never knew that one night
I watched him from my window,
After his day's chores were finished.
He sat on the grass, staring at the moon
Smiling just beyond the mountains.

—Lee, grade 11

This poem seems to have taken the author by surprise. She had been on a foreign exchange program in France where she took a photography class. She took many shots of local people and came to reevaluate this subject only after forcing herself to examine her own photo of him more carefully. The division here seems to be between her old view of the subject ("always," "never") and the changed view ("that one night"). The subject, who at first seemed merely moody and distant, seems pensive and philosophical on closer inspection.

Family Reunion

She seems dwarfed, standing next to me.
Her smile spans her face like a bridge, from cheek to cheek.
Her deep brown eyes glisten through those square
bifocals that seem to get thicker every year.
You all gaze at my (now) blond hair, jaws dropped in awe.
The silver crescent moon of my grandmother's face
To the right yearns to be part of the picture.
Her red and white floral blouse could have popped out of a
    50's family sitcom. What could I possibly be staring at
Across the road? What could be interesting enough to take my
    eyes off the camera?

Across the road, horses whinny in a small yard
Bordered by a four-foot wire fence that could've been busted
    by a powerful steed. Behind me stands the small
White Barnett Ridge Church, which has a service every Sunday
    at 10:00, and swelters well above 100 degrees in the summer.
Behind the church is the Barnett Ridge cemetery.

> This cemetery is a beautiful small green fenced in plot of land
> Where my grandfather and most of my other relatives
> Are buried. Far down the road is a red abandoned barn
> Which belonged to my great-grandmother, until the state
> Expanded the highway that now runs 100 yards away.
>
> —Brandon, grade 11

Brandon wrote this poem at the end of a quarter, and I never saw a later draft. The poem is full of great details, but it seems unfinished to me. The lines don't yet break to greatest effect, and the rhetorical questions that end stanza 1 are implied by the opening of stanza 2. Also, the language seems a bit padded (several lines could be condensed a great deal). The underlined passage, for example, might become "My grandfather and most of my other relatives are buried in a small green fenced-in cemetery behind the church." But while this draft feels rough, the material is so rich—the whinnying horses, the barn, the highway that has overshadowed the pastoral scene—that this poem has always stayed with me.

In Times Of . . .

> In times of white gloves and white chiffon
> she walks toward the wall,
> her back turned to the world,
> alone.
>
> In times of long necklaces and white pearly high heels
> she walks with her head held high
> hand digging deeply in her pockets
> to keep warm.
>
> In times of petit-fours and the consistency of church on Sundays
> she carries herself with the glamour of a movie star
> while she follows the push of the wind away from the camera
> shy.
>
> In times when black and white only existed
> when color never filled in the missing spots
> the memories always appeared smudged if they appeared at all.
> Those times are over; we all must walk away.
>
> —Amy, grade 11

This poem is nicely unified by the repetition of the introductory phrase the author also uses as her title. Even though the poem is told in the third person, it reads like an "I remember" poem told from the point of view of the subject (Amy's grandmother). Here the speaker fondly reimagines her grandmother's past, yet in an amazing moment of empathy, she learns that she, like her grandmother (two generations older), must "walk away" from this notion of the past.

"Without memory we would have no sense of our own identity" (11) Garry Wills says in *Saint Augustine's Memory.* To some extent, we are our past, and therefore memory is a rich mine to tap for all artists. Exploring their memories helps students discover who they are, what they can and cannot remember, and *how* they remember the people, places, events, and ideas that have shaped their lives. Perhaps it will even affect the way they will remember future events.

7 Sounds, Speeds, and Sliding Doors

Epitaph for a Sky Diver
for the memory of J. L.

The sun, like a new dime,
burned in the pocket of sky
while he fell like a penny
pitched with a wish down a well.

—Ted Kooser

Why is this brief poem so powerful? The sounds here—all those short vowels in the final line, for example—end the poem in a rush, imitative of the freefall perhaps. Only the word *down* contains a long vowel in this line. The speed of the poem also packs a punch. Not only is this a very short poem, but the lines are short as well. And consider the punctuation. The two commas in the first line slow the reader down for a second. Then the final three lines whiz by in a hurry.

Most people take little, if any, time out of their day to consider the sounds in their world. To make sense of the world, we attend to a dominant sound or two and allow the rest of the world to fade into the background. Nor do most people consider time as anything more than something to cope with—keeping appointments, meeting deadlines, negotiating traffic. In this chapter, I present activities that ask students to attend to the sounds and pacing of their everyday lives more fully than they have before.

In order to convey their experiences to their readers, students try to capture events as they occurred—as they sounded and at the pace(s) at which they ran. Specifically, we consider how the sounds of words can affect readers and how the pace of a poem (line length, punctuation, spacing) can affect meaning. At the end of the chapter, I discuss how we use these tools to write poems that imagine alternative personal histories, lives we might have lived.

Sound Poems

As a warm-up to writing sound poems, I divide the class in two (or, with large classes, into smaller groups) and have each student choose a different sound, a single syllable, that connotes tranquility. Making sure that everyone can be heard, they perform their sounds to the rest of the class. We discuss why some sounds seem pleasant to our ears and try to make hypotheses as to why these sounds are so appealing. Why is "Ahhhh" more relaxing than, say, "Eeeek"? The short vowel in the first? The harsh consonant in the second?

My students and I also play a slightly longer (and somewhat noisier!) game in which small groups use actual words to evoke a place: a pond, a computer lab, a dry cleaning store, a campfire. Kids love to perform these scenes for one another. It's especially fun to notice how they order their words. A group of middle school students performed this pond poem: "fish splash wish wash drip dapple ripple." These words suggest a great deal of activity at the pond. I like the way they put the "sh" words together at the beginning and the "p" words at the end. Their words evoke pond life more vividly than merely telling the reader about a "noisy pond." Similarly words such as *ticket* or *data* might capture the sounds of a computer lab better than more literal computer words such as *mouse* or *modem*.

We then read two sound poems—Paul Simon's "Changing Opinion" and Sylvia Plath's "Cinderella"—and discuss the sound patterns in each.

Changing Opinion

Gradually
We became aware
Of a hum in the room
An electrical hum in the room
It went MMMMMMM

We followed it
From corner to corner
We pressed our ears
Against the wall
We crossed diagonals
And put our hands on the floor
It went MMMMMMM

Sometimes it was a murmur
Sometimes it was a pulse
Sometimes it seemed to disappear
But then with a quarter turn of the head
It would roll around the sofa,
A nimbus humming cloud
MMMMMMM

Maybe it's the hum
Of a calm refrigerator
Cooling on a big night
Maybe it's the hum of our parents' voices
Long ago in a soft light
MMMMMMM

Maybe it's the hum
Of a changing opinion
Or a foreign language in prayer
Maybe it's the mantra
Of the walls and wiring
Deep breathing
Soft air
MMMMMMM

Most sounds live in the background of our lives as white noise, a sonic canvas to which we usually pay little attention. After listening to this poem, my students love listening to "silence." If they take a minute to listen carefully, they can hear that background music—the sound of the fluorescent lights in our classroom, the wind and the trees and the birds outside. (Luckily for me, this lasts for only a minute, or we'd never get anything done all year.)

Aside from the solid "MMMM" lines in the Simon poem, I ask students to hear how the language functions on two levels—description and sound. Together, for example, we list the nasal consonants (hum, room, murmur, nimbus, maybe, mantra; changing opinion, foreign language; walls wiring), all of which imitate the "electrical hum."

Cinderella

The prince leans to the girl in scarlet heels,
Her green eyes slant, hair flaring in a fan
Of silver as the rondo slows; now reels
Begin on tilted violins to span

The whole revolving tall glass palace hall
Where guests slide gliding into lights like wine;
Rose candles flicker on the lilac wall
Reflecting in a million flagons' shine,

And gilded couples in a whirling trance
Follow holiday revel begun long since,
Until near twelve the strange girl all at once
Guilt-stricken halts, pales, clings to the prince

> As amid the hectic music and cocktail talk
> She hears the caustic ticking of the clock.

Plath's amazing poem (which she wrote as a teenager) is always a favorite. As with "Changing Opinion," I ask students to identify the poem's sound patterns and to suggest how those patterns are functioning. Students first notice the abab rhymes (the last word rhymes in lines 1 and 3 and in lines 2 and 4 within each stanza). And students quickly point out that this regular pattern seems consistent with the setting of the poem: a dance. Look at the short *i*'s in line 4; the series of long *i*'s in line 6; the *l*'s in lines 7 and 8; and, perhaps most conspicuously, the ticking noises in the final lines—all those *t* and *k* sounds! Consistent with the narrative of the poem, the speaker is acutely aware of the time. Everything will change at midnight. I ask students what difference it would make in the poem if line 11 read "Until near midnight the girl suddenly . . . ." This line says nearly the same thing denotatively, but connotatively the sounds of the words "Until near twelve the strange girl all at once"—those four *t* sounds—reinforce the inevitable progression toward the end of the dance, the end of the magic spell.

Now students are ready to write their own sound poems. I ask them to choose an event with a dominant sound. Ideally students would all make up their own topics, but I have no problem suggesting topics that have worked well for students in the past: light rain, making popcorn, a thunderstorm, electrical appliances, a ping-pong game, a fried breakfast, any race against time, pruning a garden. For this assignment, I ask students to write poems that are a minimum of six lines long and that use a minimum of eight sounds to imitate the subject of the poem. (These numbers are somewhat arbitrary, but students are comforted by concrete expectations, and they can always increase or reduce the repetition of sounds as they revise.)

Here are some poems my students have written:

Geometry and My Death

I thought I knew it all:
Trapezoids, triangles, cubes, and cones.
It was a test against time.
As the clock ticked, my arms felt pricked by needle points.
I ran for the exit; I wanted to shout.
The echo of re-take already in my ears.

—Elliot, grade 8

This short poem uses terms from a geometry test for their sonic value (those *t* and *c* and *k* sounds) to show how the ticking clock on a timed test overwhelms the speaker's concentration. I love the phrase "echo of re-take" in the final line which recalls all the previous *k* sounds.

Rain

Raindrops plopping in the street.
Pedestrians leaping over puddles,
Pushing through the sloshing storm.
Bombarding raindrops,
Falling in parabolas,
Pelting passers-by.
Raindrops plopping in the street.

—Alex, grade 8

This poem nicely establishes the rain sound with the repetition of the *p* sounds at the beginning, middle, and end of words. I think the most satisfying sounds come in unexpected words (*bombard, parabola*) rather than in more obvious words like *plopping*, though the bookend effect of the first and last lines works well here.

Drone

Hissssssssssssss

A drop of sweat hits the sun-black asphalt

A cat wilts in the yard next door

Condensation evaporates on the tar on the roof

Ssssssssshhhhh

An unscrewed fire hydrant gushes on the west side

A freshwater wave hits limestone at the point

A shopkeeper hoses down his dusty walk

Pssssssssssstttttt

Park district campers tell sweaty secrets under slides

Spray cans release dreams of the cool

An exhausted mother scolds her baby

Sssswwiiiissshh

Melting ice makes moves in lemonade

Her skirt dances with her ankles

Zzzzzzzzzzzzzz

The bugs like kazoos

The laundry vent releases sweet steam

An old man snores with his whole body in the park

Beneath the sirens and screams, silhouettes of sounds drone their
  dirge.

The city will not relent until the silence of its cold.

—Michael, grade 12

This poem delights in summer sounds. The author uses an effective
blend of onomatopoetic sounds and beautiful descriptions that recap-
ture those sounds (the Hssss followed by *hits* and *asphalt;* the Zzzzzz
followed by *bugs* and *kazoos*). The poem's organization also underscores
the importance of sounds: sounds of summer street life resound until
winter hits with the "silence of [the] cold" in the final line.

Manumission

water flows slowly
  filling the rich,
    silver wet river
      cresting in manumission
                    COARSE ROAR
        sudden, hungry, rushing, thunder
      bright fire stripes strike
    the liberating ship arrives
  racing waves
praying slaves

—Adrienne, grade 11

Here's a sound poem on a much more serious topic—slave liberation.
The poet hears the beautiful sound of the roiling waters that lead to freedom in the word *manumission,* sounds not found in the word *emancipa-
tion,* for example. Further, she offers pairs of words with common vowel
sounds in the opening lines, culminating in the capitalized midpoint of
the poem. Perhaps she intends this line to be shouted, to be roared. I
love the clear patterns here, such as the repeated long *i* sounds in line 7
and the long *a* pattern in the final two lines. This poet uses spacing to

great effect (perhaps indicative of people leaving one place and finding a new home, or the push of a boat through the water—a wave, the
wake). Students consider spacing further in the speed poems that follow.

Speed Poems

Like sound poems, speed poems attempt to show readers an event without explicitly telling them about that event. Rather, they let the length
of syllables and lines, the punctuation, and the spacing suggest the speed
at which the event took place. A poem that captures the speed of an event
also guides how the poem will be read (a feature discussed again in
Chapter 10, which focuses on reading poems for performance).

Let's return to Plath's "Cinderella" poem on pages 64 and 65.
While the line length remains fairly consistent throughout, an important shift occurs at the end of the poem. The abab structure breaks down
and the poem ends with a rhymed couplet (two consecutive rhyming
lines). This furthers the idea of the magic spell breaking suddenly and
abruptly for Cinderella. Punctuation is also used judiciously in this
poem. Why, for example, is there a semicolon in line 3? This marker
slows down the poem, just as the "rondo slows" in the poem's narrative. Look at the two commas in line 12. These markers capture the halt-
ing, stuttering Cinderella as she anxiously ponders her next move.

One especially good source of speed poem models is *Motion:
American Poems about Sport* because many of the poems feature writing
that imitates sporting actions: serve and volley tennis; slalom skiing;
swimming races, and so on. My other favorite models are Edward
Hirsch's "Fast Break" and Dick Lourie's "What It's Like Living in Ithaca,
New York":

Fast Break
In memory of Dennis Turner, 1946–1984

A hook shot kisses the rim and
hangs there, helplessly, but doesn't drop,

and for once our gangly starting center
boxes out his man and times his jump

perfectly, gathering the orange leather
from the air like a cherished possession

and spinning around to throw a strike
to the outlet who is already shoveling

an underhand pass toward the other guard
scissoring past a flat-footed defender

who looks stunned and nailed to the floor
in the wrong direction, trying to catch sight

of a high, gliding dribble and a man
letting the play develop in front of him

in slow motion, almost exactly
like a coach's drawing on the blackboard,

both forwards racing down court
the way that forwards should, fanning out

and filling the lanes in tandem, moving
together as brothers passing the ball

between them without a dribble, without
a single bounce hitting the hardwood

until the guard finally lunges out
and commits to the wrong man

while the power-forward explodes past them
in a fury, taking the ball into the air

by himself now and laying it gently
against the glass for a lay-up,

but losing his balance in the process,
inexplicably falling, hitting the floor

with a wild, headlong motion
for the game he loved like a country

and swiveling back to see an orange blur
floating perfectly through the net.

—Edward Hirsch

"Fast Break," though forty lines long, is told in a single sentence. Hirsch is imitating the speed, grace, and fluidity of a perfectly executed fast break in this poem. He keeps the action moving with a minimum of punctuation, just as a good point guard would push the ball up the court hard, keeping the defenders on their heels and not allowing them a chance to catch up.

What It's Like Living in Ithaca, New York

here's what it's like: let's say you have just had
lunch someplace in Collegetown and you are
on your way to Karl Yentz's garage with
your VW because yesterday you noticed the brakes were
   beginning

                                                                    to fade

you start down Buffalo Street hill   it
looks like rain now after a sunny morning:
when you slow down for the blinking yellow
light at Stewart Avenue those brakes are
not good

            and it gets worse   that huge old green
house on the corner of Fountain Place and
then the shiny face of Terrace Hill Apartments
flash by you like the past   you feel terror
in your wrists   your stomach   and you know
those brakes are gone and you won't be able
to stop at the red light on Aurora

where there are several people leisurely
crossing your path: maybe on their way from
the Unitarian Church to Hal's
Delicatessen or they just left their
own apartment to go buy some flowers
or whatever errands you do all day—
in any case there they are and you can't stop

so this is what it's like: as if your brakes
had failed and you couldn't avoid running
right through that crowd knocking them all apart—
panic   broken limbs   and screams in the street

well the chances are that on any
given day at least one of these people
would be somebody you had quarreled with
last year and hadn't spoken to since   or
a friend you had visited only last week
or even the person you were married to yourself

who would see just before impact   that it was you
that's what it's like living in Ithaca.

                                                   —Dick Lourie

Lourie's poem uses an unconventional device—a car headed down a hill with no brakes. Like such a car, this poem picks up speed as it moves along. It uses a minimum of punctuation as well as unconventional spacing that might disorient the reader just as the disoriented driver struggles to regain his equilibrium.

Writing Speed Poems

As with other poems, I encourage students to choose their own topics, but some topics that have consistently worked well are train rides, passing periods in school, stop-and-go traffic, roller coasters, elevators, bike riding, and many actions in sports. I suggest writing poems that contain a change of pace unless students are trying to imitate a single great rush, as in Hirsch's poem. The only other caution I offer is that poems that try to imitate something sluggish and boring (a car that won't start, being stopped dead in traffic, for example) run the risk of the mimetic fallacy: If it was boring to live through, it is likely to be boring to read.

I encourage students to experiment with different spacing, fonts, and arrangements of words on the page in order to imitate the pace of the topic. Many students love the freedom this allows, and they often present poems with daring and originality; it is also gratifying to see how well they incorporate sound patterns into their speed poems. Here are a few examples of my students' work:

Jazz

is

the juking j i v e of hips   a c r o s s   a Harlem
               juke
                 joint
The   Rhythm   and   Rhyme
Of the guitar player
PromptlyPLUCKING perfectlyPITCHEDtones
    while his fingers do a Latin merengue dance
     A   c   r   o   s   s
The fingerboard
   The **DRUMMMMMMMMMMMMMER** C H O P S on his
Snare with   lightning
        Speed c
         u
         t
         t

                                        i
                                     n
                                  g through the tonal vibes of
                                    his ride cymbal
              while emphasizing the consistent m e t r o n o m e like
                  "<u>chick</u>" of his high hat
              bouncing up
                          and
                                    down
              paving
                      a beat of
                                  solid gold soul for the
              Trumpet to blast past with a melodic C O O L co nf using
                  melee flowing up
              and
                      down   in   and   out of scales while the

                          basic Boss tone Boomin   Bass
              throws down a **heavy   s l o p p y** swingingphatafrocuban
                                  R   H   Y   T   H   M
                                                              Which the
                          E   V   S
              Piano W   A   E   in and out of, effortlessly singing
                  its lovely, ladylike
              linguistic lingo

                          Over
                          And
                                  Over
              While the Singer
              W A I L S   **WILD** wicked woes Skeebops and boo's
                  While   M i X i N g all of
              the instruments together in   one
              Voice

                                              —Brandon, grade 11

This poem must have been as fun to write as it is to read aloud. The
poet had read e. e. cummings's "Buffalo Bill's" the week before writing
this poem, and this may account for some of the passages in which
words run into one another. From the first two sizzling words *jazz is*,
it's clear that sounds will matter in this poem. The syncopation in the

line "The Rhythm and Rhyme" is great, and the outstretched fingers of the guitarist across the fingerboard is a wonderful choice.

I always speak in terms of a writer's choices, but it's especially important with these poems. I want to encourage students to take chances and to write in ways they never have before. Why, I might ask, for example, has the poet not chosen to run the phrase "Snare with lightning speed" together? I don't necessarily think this is a mistake, but I want students to consider why poets have made the choices they've made. Regardless of this poet's justifications, I think this is a wonderful poem full of amazing sounds and great attention to pacing throughout.

Rowboat

Ripples and	waves
Weighty oars held	by a small boy
Yawning-yellow rays	glow on the lake
Cove after cove	bay after bay
The Woods	on shore
Harbor childish	imaginations:
Of savage natives,	famous adventurers,
Like those	which lured
The youth	on this journey
A melancholy	postcard:
The small boat,	the sad boy
The setting sun	glowing orange,
He glides endlessly	over the water
His swollen face	moist with tears
Glances around	one last time
For the	wooden cabin
Home	

—Sylvain, grade 11

This poem is beautifully shaped like the prow of the eponymous rowboat. The clever two-column structure allows the poem to be read in waves, or in starts and stops (like oar strokes?) that get quicker and quicker as the poem concludes, as the boat reaches home.

Anticipation

> Orlando Hernandez stands on the rubber.
>> Takes a deeeeeep breath. Exhales.
>>> Checks the catcher's sign,
>>>> Nods,
> He steps back, starts his patented "El Duque" windup,
>> Pivots,
> Brings his arm over his head,
>> Lifts his leg
>>> Kicks it forward,
>>>> And steps toward the catcher.
>> His arm straightens
>>> Side-arm now
>>>> He reaches toward the plate
>>>>> and lets go

—Brian, grade 11

This poem begins slow and gets faster once the pitcher is in his windup. The author writes the word *deep* with extra letters so that the reader is forced to hang on the long *e* sound even longer, and he uses three sentences in the first two lines to underscore Hernandez's slow, careful preparation. The next sentence lasts eight lines. This poem also takes advantage of word placement on the page: the poem's shape seems to imitate the pitcher's contortions, and the final word, *go*, appears all the way over on the right margin, highlighting the anticipation connected with the release of the baseball.

In sound and speed poems, students tried to present actions and events as they occurred. In the poems highlighted in the next section, students capture the sounds and speeds of events as they *might* have occurred.

Sliding Doors Poems

What parent or teacher hasn't said, "Actions have consequences"? The following exercise explores this idea by considering the consequences of enormously significant or apparently trivial actions. Whereas students considered their unaltered past lives through poems focused on memories and photographs (see Chapter 6), this exercise asks students to imagine how their lives would be different if they had acted differently.

Reconsidering the past—either wallowing in regret or counting our blessings—is something many people do when they think about their past. As Dana Gioia puts it in his poem "Summer Storm," "Memory insists on pining / For places it never went, / As if life would be happier / Just by being different." Though this assignment takes its title from the popular movie *Sliding Doors* starring Gwyneth Paltrow, I got the idea when I read the following two poems from two different collections on the same night:

Sun-Times

Walking down the apartment hall
I saw a 35-cent Chicago Sun-Times
on the floor in front of a tenant's door
I was tempted to steal it
but I thought some more:
If I take that 35-cent newspaper
the tenant will hold a grudge
and talk back to his boss
who will in turn fire him.
And he will go back home
and try to find another job unsuccessfully
and he will get resentful and beat his wife
day and night until she can't take it anymore.
And she will shoot him dead to save her life,
but most likely, the judge being a man,
to save his gender's face
will give her 99 years.
And meanwhile their little son
will be sent in tears to an orphanage
where he will grow up secretly psychotic
but with some luck will be befriended
by the Democratic Precinct Captain
who plays Santa Claus every Christmas
And he will get into politics and graduate
from law school, still a fool
but with a lot of clout.
Then he'll become an Alderman
Then Chicago's mayor
Then Illinois Governor
Then he'll become president . . .
Then one morning at the White House, when his aide

brings him the morning world newspapers
he will realize that one is missing
and he will start cussing and hissing
just like his daddy
and he will blame the Russians
and before you know it
he will push the red button sending off
huge atomic missiles
and Russia will retaliate
and the whole world will blow up
and then we'll all be dead!
> So I left the newspaper
> by the door instead.

> —David Hernandez

Many students love the playful rhymes that sound throughout this poem. I think it's also important to show that poetry does not always take itself so seriously; poems can be funny. Throughout most of the poem, Hernandez's speaker fantasizes a chain of improbable consequences his action would set into motion. He waits until the very end to make his crucial decision to *not* steal the newspaper. A change of pace at the end of the poem, a strategy used by some students in their speed poems, sets off the final two lines to highlight their importance, the way students might in their speed poems.

I Go Back to the House for a Book

I turn around on the gravel
and go back to the house for a book,
something to read at the doctor's office,
and while I am inside, running the finger
of inquisition along a shelf,

another me that did not bother
to go back to the house for a book
heads out on his own,
rolls down the driveway,
and swings left toward town,

a ghost in his ghost car,
another knot in the string of time,
a good three minutes ahead of me—
a spacing that will now continue
for the rest of my life.

Sometimes I think I see him
a few people in front of me on a line
or getting up from a table
to leave the restaurant just before I do,
slipping into his coat on the way out the door.

But there is no catching him,
no way to slow him down
and put us back into sync,
unless one day he decides to go back
to the house for something,

but I cannot imagine
for the life of me what that might be.
He is out there always before me,
blazing my trail, invisible scout,
hound that pulls me along,

shade I am doomed to follow,
my perfect double,
only bumped an inch into the future,
and not nearly as well-versed as I
in the love poems of Ovid—

I who went back to the house
that fateful winter morning and got the book.

                              —Billy Collins

I like the fact that Collins's poem differs from Hernandez's poem in almost every way. For starters, this poem doesn't rhyme. Also, the speaker makes his crucial decision very early in the poem. The speaker has a much more stately tone; this speaker goes back for a "book," after all, not a newspaper. Collins's poem is also carefully measured: each stanza has five lines—until the end. Collins, too, uses a change of pace at the end, emphasizing his "fateful" decision in the final couplet.

Students love this assignment and they respond to it in very different ways—absurdly funny, like Hernandez, or thoughtfully and seriously, like Collins. It's important to validate both choices. There is a place for humor in poetry that all too often goes unrecognized.

Since I assign the sliding doors poem right after the sound and speed poems, I ask students to incorporate what they've learned into these poems. They try to convey the sounds of the actions being described through the sounds of their own language. The climax of sliding doors poems—the moment when a speaker decides whether to act—is often tense and pressure filled. This is a good opportunity to signal the tension and anxiety through shorter lines, alternative spacing, and/or intruding punctuation.

Here are a few student examples:

Emotionally Repressed Pizza Man

I said "Hi" to a pizza man in my elevator today.
  As I entered my apartment
I thought, "What would have happened if I hadn't?"
    Maybe he wouldn't have cared,
        Or, maybe . . .
He would have angrily stalked out of the elevator,
    The glower on his face securing him a lower tip.
Then, exiting the building, a tenant would let the door slam
    in his face,
Igniting a searing pain from a cockfighting wound he had
  acquired in his youth.
    Rage mounting, he'd back out of the driveway
        With a quick, powerful thrust of the gas pedal,
    Hitting the approaching BMW 606RHU with tremendous
        force.
After being informed by the driver that a lawsuit was coming,
        He would speed back to Domino's.
    Arriving in a huff, his not-so-pleasant boss
        Would hastily remind him he was 20 minutes late.
At this point the pizza man would lose it:
            GRAB A HOT PIZZA PAN OUT OF THE
OVEN AND KNOCK HIS BOSS UNCONSCIOUS WITH IT. HIS
NEXT VICTIM, IN REVERSE-CHRONOLOGICAL-ORDER WOULD
BE THE BMW DRIVER, ROLLED OVER BY THE DELIVERY CAR.
AFTER DISPATCHING OF HIM, HIS COCKFIGHTING NERVES
WOULD KICK IN AND INSPIRE HIM TO SEEK REVENGE ON THE
MISCREANT WHO HAD NOT HELD THE DOOR FOR HIM. ONCE
INSIDE THE BUILDING, HE'D SEEK OUT THE LOUSY TIPPER
AND. . . .

At this point in my mental deliberations, I thought,
    Thank God for common courtesy.

—Roberto, grade 11

This poem is funny and wild, which the uneven lines help to reveal. The speaker goes on a rant near the end, switching to all capital letters, as he loses himself in the fever of his dream, until he recovers his equilibrium in the final two lines.

Orphan

If I had been a 20-year-old man
when the Korean War broke out,
I'm sure I would have joined the army.

I would hear mother's crying all night
lying on my bed, looking at the stars,
and smelling their scent on my cheek.

My whole family would come to the train station
to say good-bye to me already on the train
with short hair and the uniform on.

Families outside would wave flags
and handkerchiefs, and their young sons
inside would wave their hats.

A loud steam blast.
The train separates us from us.
I let go of my mother's two-handed grip.

She fades into the thick and white steam
Waving her handkerchief.
I smell the scent of stars on my cheek again.

I see a man coming out from the front car.
He looks like a real soldier, and his voice, too.
He speaks so loud that my left ear's going to blow up.

I try my best to remember his words
not to be lost in the battle,
not to be lost in a foggy day.

I am in the middle of the battle right now . . .
Suddenly shooting started, so I started shooting, too.
However, I don't know where I am aiming.

                                    —Kwan-mo, grade 11

This poem is a powerful imagining of what it would have been like to be born fifty years earlier. Drawing on discussions with older relatives who fought in the war, the author re-creates an amazingly poignant—

and almost cinematic—farewell scene at the train station. I love the way this poem ends in the present tense. The speaker is so caught up in his own vivid reverie that he is disoriented and no longer knows the country or even century in which he is living.

The Escapade

Looking into the mirror
Of the dressing room
In Marshall Field's on State St.,
I think about stealing this sky blue
Silk shirt by Liz Claiborne.
I could easily hide it, I think,
Under my baggy U of C sweatshirt
As I swiftly make my way
Toward the exit
The alarm sounds,
All eyes turn on me
I spin around
Two bulky security guards
March my way.
Cold metal cuffs
Wrap my wrists,
And I am shoved
Into a leather-seated squad car
With sirens wailing loudly.
My head is spinning . . . I don't know where I'm going. . . .

I put the shirt back on the hanger.
Only then do I realize it's me
Still looking in the mirror
Of the Marshall Field's dressing room.

—Nicole, grade 11

This poem divides into two sections: the fantasy and the decision *not* to steal a shirt. The author captures some fitting sounds: the sibilant *s*'s in lines 4 and 5 and the hard *c*'s in the "cold metal cuffs." The pacing is also effective. I like the two very short sentences in the middle as the speaker imagines herself being caught: "The alarm sounds. / All eyes turn on me." In an earlier draft she had written, "All eyes suddenly turn on me." After consideration, the author realized that suddenness is implied in the shorter sentence.

Miss Teen USA, 2001

Saturday, while eating my lunch
In a downtown restaurant,
I suddenly realized I was slouching.
Should I sit up straight?
I thought to myself,
"What if the lady sitting next to me
Is a scout for the Miss Teen USA pageant?"
She just might think I have the potential
To be a contestant.

> I'll compete against girls from all over the country
> And play Mozart's *Turkish March* as my special talent.
> For the evening gown competition, I'll wear a black dress
> With diamond sequins across the front, and one of those
> Famous white sashes that will read "MISS ILLINOIS."

> When it comes down to the final question—
> How should America respond to terrorist attacks?—
> I'll answer just the way the judges want me to.
> I'll explain that we should confront the terrorists peacefully
> Because world peace is what I care about above all else.

> The judges will narrow their selection to a final three . . .
> 2nd runner-up, Miss Wyoming.
> 1st runner-up, Miss Tennessee.

> And your Miss Teen USA 2001 is . . .
> Miss Illinois!
> Here I go, walking and waving,
> Standing up straight to balance my crown.

So, I decide not to slouch
Until the lady sitting next to me
Silently walks out.

—Caitlin, grade 10

This poem uses speed nicely in imitating the drama of the runners-up, and the ellipses and the short sentences capture the sense of anticipation. I really like the author's decision to move the "fantasy" lines to the right. The speaker's return to reality in the end is signaled by the switch back to the left margin.

Through sound, speed, and sliding door poems, we not only explore our lives through poetry, but we also experiment with poetic tools—sound patterns, punctuation, spacing, fonts—to relate our lives to our readers. As with earlier exercises, most of the material comes from our own lives (the sounds and tempos of our lives and the lives we might have led). The next chapter explores how we can mine the world around us to invent new poetic subjects. But because our perceptions and pre-dilections also reveal who we are, our subjects will always be, to some degree, ourselves.

8 Reading Ourselves away from Ourselves

I see all of us reading ourselves away from ourselves,
straining in circles of light to find more light
until the line of words becomes a trail of crumbs
that we follow across a page of fresh snow;

when evening is shadowing the forest
and small birds flutter down to consume the crumbs,
we have to listen hard to hear the voices
of the boy and his sister receding into the woods.

—Billy Collins, from "Books"

Even when we're not writing about our selves per se, we are writing about ourselves. The words we use are "ours"; they suggest our attitudes, our values, and our experiences. I remind my students of this all the time, particularly when they say they can't think of anything to write about, or when they complain that they have other classes in addition to English.

Many students tell me they feel scared about beginning, frozen by the tundra of a bare white sheet of paper in front of them. Often they tell me they can't think of anything *important* to say. This happens when students think they must invent their writing subjects whole within their heads instead of exploring the text of their lives, their everyday experiences. Sometimes we need to read ourselves away from ourselves, using the world around us as a text toward self-understanding.

In this chapter, I present activities that allow students to use their experiences in other classes and their experiences outside of school to adopt different personae—speaking as works of art and as historical and literary characters who cannot speak for themselves. This chapter also highlights poems in which students give voice to cities and neighborhoods, personifying the personalities of important places in their lives.

Responding to Art

When we take trips to local museums (or when my students take field trips in other classes), I ask students to select a work that speaks to them in some way, and to take this phrase literally: I want the art *to speak*. Most frequently, I ask students to adopt the persona of the work of art (especially with sculptures) or to choose a character within a painting and to write a poem in that person's voice. I am lucky enough to teach in a large city with many museums, but this activity works anywhere with galleries of any size. Field trips to museums are squarely within Dewey's vision of ideal education, helping to achieve his goal of making life inside the classroom "reflect the life of the larger society" (*School* 29).

After a middle school trip to the Oriental Institute (a museum on the campus of the University of Chicago), I asked students who had never studied Egypt to respond in the voice of the artworks they saw. I tried to focus their attention on a single piece, a single attitude, offering some general guidance: Imagine that the artwork you focus on is a person. What kind of person is this? Is the person male or female? How old is the person? Is this person strong or weak? What kind of life has this person led? How does this person feel about himself or herself? In what regard was this person held during his or her own time? How is this person regarded now? How do museum visitors see this person? How does this person feel about being in a museum? How does this person feel in general? What mood is he or she in? This last question is especially important in striking an attitude and setting a tone for the poem.

Further, I encouraged students to use the information plates next to the pieces of art they were writing about. These plates often contain biographical and historical information that can be useful in writing a persona poem.

One such information plate read:

> Helmet-like coverings were placed directly over the wrapped head and shoulders of the mummy in order to replicate the facial features for eternity. These head-pieces were often accompanied by coverings for the chest, legs and feet. Cartonnage—a substance like papier-mâché made of layers of linen and plaster—was used as a cover. Faces of cartonnage head covers were usually gilded because it was thought the deceased was associated with the sun god whose flesh was gold.

Using the text of this plate and his own interaction with the artifact, a student wrote this poem:

Egypt for the Cartoon Age

Today I am just a cartoon age *cartonnage*,
Layers of linen covering put on a freshly wrapped
Mummy. I really shined once upon a time,
And was much more popular.

Now I am delicate and rare.
I am an artifact
That has many stories to tell
About conquest and acquiescence.
If I had a voice, I would force
The stories through this wrap
For the rest of my days.

—BJ, grade 7

The nameplates and descriptions of artworks in museums are great resources for writers. Here the author makes a great play on words with *cartonnage,* a word he learned at the museum; he borrows the alliterative phrase "layers of linen"; he makes a comparison between the shiny gilding and the former status of the embalmed person; and he appropriates the wonderful line "conquest and acquiescence" from the neighboring plate as well.

Here is another poem generated from the same trip:

Egyptian Mask

I am an Egyptian mask,
Covering a sacred face
That holds great power.
Bright oranges and yellows,
Painted hieroglyphs, intimate designs.
I am beautiful. But, with time
I begin to fade. Less elegant,
Still inferior to the face underneath
Of which I'm a mere copy.
I have never seen sunlight.
I was made for rituals of death.
I can now safely say my pharaoh
Has passed into the afterlife,
Making a safe journey.
I am just a replica,
But I have his poise, his grace,
And his power.
I am his twin,
          reflected in gold.

—Jessica, grade 8

This student uses the word *hieroglyphs* and the phrase "intimate designs" from printed material near the artifact to anchor her narrative, and she creates a nice twist at the end of her poem, twinning the roles of mask and subject.

Historical Persona Poems

Just as research from visiting a museum helped students write the preceding poems, it is often useful to take advantage of the research students do in other classes in writing different kinds of poems. By asking students to write poems speaking in the voice and predicament of historical characters, I give them a chance to learn a great deal about a historical character and about a consistent voice in writing. The beautiful poem "Jeanne d'Arc" by Karen Fish is a great model for students to follow:

> **Jeanne d'Arc**
> May 1431
>
> The men arrived at dusk
> with torches to burn the webs from the trees.
> The well water had gone bad. And I could smell
> the bestial floor as the withered hay began
> furiously molting.
>
> And when all the lights had collapsed
> with the bruise color of morning, from the next field
> the smoke from damp grasses reached me.
> It is here I have slept wet-haired on stone.
>
> Some of the women had gone down
> into the potato cellars to hide, to breathe
> the wet air, to forget the ash that has already
> been smeared on their foreheads.
>
> Peasants like rain-worn stones look on, their grief-stunned
> faces stare. Early
> I had smelled a certain knowledge.
> When I heard Your voice the leaves were blowing over
> showing their undersides,
> the white that so often means rain.
>
> As the priests turn me into fire,
> I will say Your name three times.

Then from my breast they will say
they saw a white dove fly.

I am a fir in the gray forest,
farther than my eye can see are the guards in their clatter.
I am a fir in the gray forest dreaming
of ash, the ash beyond the common day
aching again to be green as You,

immutable, seen.

From the epigraphic date underneath the title, it is immediately clear that this portrait of Joan of Arc is drawn within a historical context. From the precise details (the potato cellars, the torches, the ashes, the fir trees) it seems certain that Fish has familiarized herself with the historical character and the historical event. But hers is not a work of history; it is a marvelously empathetic understanding of a brave woman's inextricable predicament.

The empathy that persona poems foster is one of the most important benefits of this assignment. Students must not only copy the style, the verbal tics of the speaker, but they must also step into the speaker's skin and try to understand his or her feelings and ideas.

Here is how one student, who was studying the history of the Vietnam War, responded to the assignment:

Pleiku

Their AK-47's snap off shots like small firecrackers,
Their bullets whiz by like buzzing mosquitoes.
And, over this: the occasional thud of mortar rounds
And the thunderous booms of an RPG hitting home.

The screams of anguish.
The pain of silence.
The lull of night.
The whirring of the Huey blades
Screaming inside my head.

The sounds: morning shells, nighttime bombardments,
the clanging bottles of Jack Daniels.
And the sounds you don't hear, you could never hear:
The whiz of the round that will injure you.
The whine of the shell that will kill you.
The zip of the body bag closing over your head.

—Amar, grade 12

This student uses military terms to great advantage, adding verisimilitude to his poem, but he also captures the abject terror of the war that pervades so many accounts of Vietnam. Mining the senses, this student concentrates on the terrible sounds surrounding this soldier in Pleiku and allows the reader to see how for this soldier sounds are associated with his greatest fear: his own mortality.

Writing in the personae of historical characters can enrich a student's understanding of both disciplines. When a class of eighth graders in an interdisciplinary American Studies class was studying immigration, they read a number of first-person accounts and some broader historical treatments of why people emigrated, what they hoped to find in America, and what they gained and lost in the process. I asked students to write as the historical figures they had studied or to create a representative figure from a certain country and write from that person's perspective. Since these poems often told complicated narratives, they tended to be rather long. Here are snatches of several poems:

Ireland

Once there were green fields,
Once there were healthy crops,
Once there was peace.
Now people scream of new ideas
In a country free of the English,
And the fields outside have turned red with blood.

Like flocks of birds sensing danger,
People fled from our country,
To this new America, and I fled with them.
But, people were cruel in this "golden land."
They barked out names, "mick," "potato eater,"
And I was forced to work in a factory 10 hours a day
Just to survive the starvation and the cold.
Smoke filled my lungs like a dry tornado,
But I kept quiet at work, afraid someone would hear
How I spoke and laugh one of those big American-
hyena laughs.

—Drew, grade 8

Greece

My country was a land
Rich in history and golden soil.
The smell of salt air everywhere,

The warm sun on my back.
We were poor but happy.
When we arrived in America,
And saw the Statue of Liberty,
I cried for my new freedom, my new home,
My new life. . . .

—Cynthia, grade 8

[Untitled]

I remember a colorful world,
Familiar faces in the marketplace,
Greeting me with a smile.
And how is your father today, Yentl?
I smile and nod. *He's well.*
Smells rise up to greet my nose,
Freshly baked challah, smoked meat.
Standing by a fire, the town elders
Huddle around the Rabbi in the winter cold.
Their voices carry arguments through the frigid air:
Which came first, Rabbi, the chicken or the egg?
Two women—one who birthed me, the other, my aunt—
Chatter like hens, spreading their gossip
Like honey over bread. *Did you hear?*
Moishe fell down and broke his arm.
Oyoyoy!

—Julia, grade 8

The language derived from research grounds these poems in rich specificity (the epithets: "mick," "potato eater"; the sensory impressions: salt air and freshly baked bread; and the gossipy dialogue in the final poem). Furthermore, the process of writing these persona poems teaches empathy. Students feel more deeply the powerful swirl of emotions that immigrants must have felt—the hope and optimism, the fear and regret, the sense of otherness that accompanies any member of a new minority group.

Literary Persona Poems

Students can also use their study of literary characters to write persona poems from different characters' perspectives. This is an especially good way to infer characters' unvoiced thoughts or to imagine scenes in books that occur "offstage." Since these scenes are rich in conflict (especially internal conflict), they offer good occasions for writing poems.

After studying *Macbeth,* one student wrote this poem in the voice of Lady Macbeth:

Control

I can't let go now,
Not after all I've done.
But how can I go on?
I'm afraid to close my eyes at night.
I haven't left this castle in weeks. I'm afraid
to go outside
myself.
God knows
what will happen next . . . my mind is like a runaway train. . . .
I'll write this down, so tonight I'll remember
what I have to do.

—Emily, grade 9

This student not only incorporates a quote from the play into her poem but also uses her knowledge of the play and of Lady Macbeth's controlling character to help her write the poem. Despite her anachronistic comparison to the "runaway train," her crafty line breaks are particularly revealing, emphasizing the fact that Lady Macbeth is very "afraid" and that her fear is interior—within the walls of the castle (she never leaves the castle during the play), within the walls of her own thoughts. She is also alone: the word *myself* occupies a line by itself.

Persona poems are particularly helpful in developing focus in students' poetry. The dramatic limitation of a single character facing a single critical decision helps students stay within the dramatic moment. Sometimes when students imitate the diction of the speaker, these poems also offer neat minilessons in word choice and registers of diction. Consider this excerpt from a student writing as George from Steinbeck's *Of Mice and Men:*

Reflections by the Salinas River

Here I am, and what do you know?
We're out of work, out of town—run out!
'Cause of Lennie I'm laid low.
(I know he'd say I take the fun out;
but then what does he know anyway?)

Poor bastard; say jump, he'll leap
And he keeps killing those stupid mice . . .
Least now, at last, he's asleep,
not causing trouble—hell is that nice.
It's just too bad he can't sleep all day.

—Katie, grade 9

This student takes a scene from the opening chapter and tries to imagine George's secret feelings, those he cannot share with Lennie. She does a nice job of speaking in George's dialect here, using casual language and contractions. In order to preserve the rhyming pattern she chose, however, she substitutes *leap* for *jump* in line 6. Discussing these choices in class, students could readily hear that *leap* is a more exaggerative word. This word choice also runs counter to the suggestion of Lennie's mechanical responses that runs throughout the novel. One student noted: "He's even called 'Machine' at one point in the novel." The poet also calls attention to the different levels of diction between George and Lennie. George would say "laid low," but he regularly lowers his diction to accommodate the slower Lennie (who'd say "take the fun out"). Writing this persona poem enabled this author to understand George's character more clearly and also helped her see the persona George wore in front of Lennie—the person with whom George could act most naturally.

Writing persona poems also helps students become better readers. Jeff Wilhelm, in *"You Gotta BE the Book,"* argues that the practice of "filling in the gaps and adding meaning to text" is particularly important for less engaged readers since it forces them to be more active, "more productive and participatory," in their role as readers (138). Persona poems encourage this sort of active reading.

Dramatizing People in Our Lives

Just as we can fill in "gaps" in literature with dramatic monologues, we can foster empathy in our daily lives by trying to imagine what the people around us—the streetwise vendor, the taxicab driver, the reclusive neighbor down the street—are thinking and feeling. It is especially helpful if the poet has a chance to talk with the person in order to get an initial understanding of his or her words and attitudes; the rest must be inferred. I offer a special caveat with this assignment: students may *not* speak in the voice of another teacher or student in the school. Words can wound, and this rule helps keep the classroom safe for sharing our lives and our language.

Here is a lovely poem by a girl who imagines her father shun-
ning his family life on an Irish farm for a life different from the one his
father led:

Daddy

I wake before the sun,
In the damp darkness,
My bare feet hitting the cold floor,
My skin prickling in the morning air.
My father is outside already,
Preparing the tractor.
I dress and stumble out the door,
Grab the tin pail,
The icy handle clinking
With each step I take toward the barn.

I hurry to milk the cows
Dig the turf,
Feed the pigs,
Collect the spuds,
And clean them.

The sun appears slowly over the horizon,
Each new ray promising rescue.
I trudge off to school when my chores are done,
Knowing my eyes will shut unwillingly
During Latin lessons,
And I will have my knuckles rapped
In front of the class.
But I have followed my heart away
From the fields.

At the four o'clock bell
I head up the road,
Through the fields
To my father.
All the time thinking,
I don't want his life.

—Nuala, grade 12

This student had heard her father talk about his life in Ireland before
coming to the United States, but here she reimagines the scene in which
he makes the decision to follow his own path. I love the early concrete

sensory descriptions and the specific list of chores in the third stanza (notice she keeps his word *spuds* instead of translating it as *potatoes*). The author captures the burden of routine in a life on the farm: the fixed order of activities, the references to the sun as a reminder of duties. The organization of the poem—a day in the life—works well here. Sunlight brings not only a respite from the chores but also the illuminating possibilities of education and learning outside the life the speaker inherited.

The next poem grew out of conversations a student had with a street person. He wanted to capture not only the words but also the desperate feelings and dreams of this person:

Monologue of the Street

I talk to the voices; they ask me questions about my past
and present. It's cold. I have to deal with the frost too
far from home too close to death. In the park, I have to deal
with death. They appear; they haunt me. Sometimes they tell
me to get a job or leave; hover around me while I sleep, bring
me food. I wasn't always like this, you know. Times used to be
different. Sometimes I have enough for liquor, if not for food. I
don't ask unless I have to. Sometimes I find food when I search
at night. To keep alive, I have to run away from the voices, but
they find me, and make me answer them. Nobody understands; they look in the opposite direction and laugh at me. You
can't understand how it is to sleep in the cold with nowhere to
go. When I get a drink, everything is good for a while, but then
it ends. I'm here again without a job or a place to stay. It's late.
I've been on the street too long. You ask me where I live? I
don't. I'm homeless.

—Mikhail, grade 12

The title of this poem is immediately surprising. It is as if the street—and not a street person—is narrating the poem. The prose poem format seems appropriate since there is very little about this person's life that is pretty or orderly. Some amazingly poignant moments have been taken from the conversation this student had with the subject of the poem: other people are referred to as "voices" (disembodied); the enjambment in line 2—"too" can be taken in both senses; the temporary relief of alcoholic stupor; and the powerful last line of homeless living as not living at all.

In *This Boy's Life,* Tobias Wolff says, "It takes a childish or corrupt imagination to make symbols of other people" (246), yet, sadly, we do this all the time without meaning to. Like the earlier persona poems, however, these poems do a great deal to foster empathy between poets and their speakers. In large part this is due to the dialogues from which these poems sprout. I love how these poems come from everyday conversations with people who figure prominently in our lives—a parent, a homeless person, a bus driver, the mail carrier—people who share our world but not necessarily our outlook. This exercise forces us to look at the people in our lives not as merely filling a role but as people.

City/Neighborhood Poems

Before the big eighth-grade class trip to Washington, D.C., one year, my class read a few poems about cities and places. We looked at Mary Chapin Carpenter's "I Am a Town," a song in which the town—a stereotypical small southern town—is the speaker. We looked at Carl Sandburg's "Chicago," a section of Toni Morrison's *Jazz* that I excerpted for its beautiful description of Harlem in the 1920s, Dar Williams's song "Southern California Wants to Be Western New York," and Yeats's "The Lake Isle of Innisfree." This wide range of styles in this mix of poems and pop song models reassures students that they can take this assignment anywhere their imaginations can take them.

We talked about how cities and other places have definite personalities and wondered whether it was possible to capture the essence of a place with words. Students loved the idea that two different views of the same city could be equally true, depending on who the speaker is and what part of the city or neighborhood the speaker belongs to.

I asked students to personify Washington, D.C., to imagine the kind of person who could represent the city, by answering the following questions:

1. Is the city a man or a woman?
2. How old is she or he?
3. How early does the person wake up?
4. What would this person eat for breakfast?
5. What kind of family life does this person have? Does she or he live alone or with relatives?
6. What kind of clothes does the person wear?
7. What kind of job does the person hold?

8. What kind of car does the person drive?
9. What kind of music does the person listen to?
10. How many friends does this person have?
11. How wealthy is this person?
12. How well educated is this person?
13. What would the person's favorite subject in school be?
14. What kind of book would this person read?
15. What is this person's favorite movie?
16. What is this person's greatest dream or aspiration?

I told students to be prepared to explain why they responded the way they did, though there is, of course, no "right" response to any item. Here are two of my students' responses and an extra credit poem a student wrote later in the year following a trip to San Francisco:

Washington Façade

She has a magnificent façade,
Amazing in its grandeur, rich in its history.
In truth, this façade masks
the filthy underbelly:
the panhandling and the crime.
She expects you to look past
poor Anacostia, past
scam-artists, past
the many homeless people
living on the street.
She does not want you to see
beyond her grand columns,
well-groomed parks,
alabaster monuments,
the clean-swept National mall.

—Lexi, grade 8

This student—like most students, for some reason—saw D.C. as a woman. I like the personifying phrase "well-groomed" that could refer to a city or a person and the attitude of this Ms. Washington who "expects" and "wants" and only offers the image of herself in return, an object to be admired.

Historian, Debater, Capital

> She dwells
> in a house built of books.
> Paper, ink, light and shade
> make vivid her home.
>
> Recording, searching, she has decided
> to become the savior of history and, herself, history.
> She preserves all which is pertinent to the past,
> having stared at, and studied the stars,
> and learned that a place hidden
>   covered in fog,
>   displaced by distance,
>   beyond our grasp,
> will preach to us its light
> long after its creation.

—Beckett, grade 8

This student sees a more bookish woman as the nation's capital. This persona is a woman who loves history and her own role in it. The tone here is less cynical, and the subject sees herself more as a beacon of truth than a mere object of beauty.

Pinwheel

> Breathe the salt from the sea—
> intoxifying the lungs from the Golden Gate Bridge
> to the sooty alleys of Chinatown.
>
> Feel the weight of your heavy eyes lift
> as the caffeine sea pumps through your veins.
>
> Fly down the street; your car has been given wings
> by the rise of bedrock below you.
> Fly free like a seagull, caressing the burning water
> of melted gold, swooping to a knoll on the delta of a river.
>
> Above the hard earth, you'll fly past pastel homes,
> and contradictions: mind and body;
> black and white; rough and smooth; bitter and sweet;
> night and day; right and wrong: they all swirl
> with verve, like a radiant pinwheel,
> spinning drunk in the salty wind.

—Pat, grade 8

Persona poems allow students to engage in pretend play with a serious purpose. Using the texts of their own lives—the books they read, the people they know, the places they visit—offers students wonderful opportunities to write. Research is easy: we can examine the world right in front of us. Furthermore, this research reminds students of the importance of focus—focusing on a particular subject and writing about that subject using specific language. This focus, in turn, invests students' writing with the power of concreteness and specificity.

By giving voice to people, places, and things that have not been given a voice, students can learn a great deal about empathy. By giving voice to their own unspoken feelings and attitudes, students can also learn a great deal about themselves: the characters they are drawn to, the objects they most cherish, the untold stories they feel are the most important to tell. We return to this work on persona in Chapter 11, where we explore the performance of poetry.

9 Writing Lives

The Next Car

Details:

A pair of red sneakers
On a train platform
Quilted in fresh snow

Serpentine cigarette smoke
Curling up
Toward a pulsing ceiling fan

A musky perfume
Leaving a murky trail
As its owner passes

Poetry
Is linking these details
Like the cars of a train,
So that as each
                    Whirs past
It compliments the first,
Passing a shimmer
Of sunlight on metal

A rhythmic rattle
Of wooden crates,

And a whisper of speed

To the next car.
            —Danielle, grade 10

In writing about poetry through the metaphor of a long commuter train she takes every day, this author makes it clear that she sees writing as part of her life, not something she does when she wants to take a break from her life. Many professional writers bristle at the idea of their "writing lives" as being somehow different from the rest of their lives. They know that their writing—the careful observation, the openness to new ideas, the exactitude of language—is already part of their lives and that writing can enrich and inform every aspect of their lives. As William Stafford has argued, "Writing itself is one of the great, free human activities," and by "working back and forth between experience and thought, writers have more than space and time can offer. They have the whole unexplored realm of human vision" (20).

This chapter explores how students can reflect on their own writing lives, first by writing poems about poetry like the poem that opens this chapter and later by revising and publishing their poetry in books. We consider two kinds of books: books written by the class and books written by individual students.

Poetry Poems

At the beginning of the year, most of my students are terrified of poetry. On interest inventories (questionnaires designed to elicit students' interests in and out of the classroom), they regularly define poetry as something they know absolutely nothing about, and they dismiss it as trivial rhyming. At best, a few describe poetry as some sort of word magic they are incapable of writing.

Having written more than twenty poems by this point in the course, however, students have more confidence in themselves as writers and more definite opinions about what poetry is and is not. So, as a culminating poetry writing exercise, I ask students to write poems about poetry. This exercise not only gives students a chance to reflect on their own writing, but it also serves as a partial course evaluation for me. How students see themselves as writers and as human beings matters a great deal to me. Are they more playful and adventurous with language than they once were? Are they more confident? Are they proud of what they have written?

Since most professional writers think of writing as an important part of their lives, many poets take up the subject of poetry as a topic to write on. Among the poetry poems I've read with students are these: Mary Oliver's "Writing Poems," Billy Collins's "Introduction to Poetry," Stephen Dunn's "A Poem Written for People Who Are Understandably Too Busy to Read Poetry," Nikki Giovanni's "Poetry," William Stafford's "Rx Creative Writing: Identity," and Donald Justice's "Poem." I'll talk about the first two of these briefly:

Writing Poems

This morning I watched
the pale green cones of the rhododendrons
opening their small pink and red blouses—

the bodies of the flowers
were instantly beautiful to the bees, they hurried
out of that dark place in the thick tree

one after another, an invisible line
upon which their iridescence caught fire
as the sun caught them, sliding down.

Is there anything more important
than hunger and happiness? Each bee entered
the frills of a flower to find

the sticky fountain, and if some dust
spilled on the walkways of the petals
and caught onto their bodies, I don't know

if the bees know that otherwise death
is everywhere, even in the red swamp
of a flower. But they did this

with no small amount of desperation—you might say: love.

And the flowers, as daft as mud, poured out their honey.

—Mary Oliver

Introduction to Poetry

I ask them to take a poem
and hold it up to the light
like a color slide

or press an ear against its hive.
I say drop a mouse into a poem
and watch him probe his way out,

or walk inside the poem's room
and feel the walls for a light switch.

I want them to water ski
across the surface of a poem
waving at the author's name on the shore.

But all they want to do
is tie the poem to a chair with rope
and torture a confession out of it.

They begin beating it with a hose
to find out what it really means.

—Billy Collins

Oliver does not mention poetry or language in her poem. She's making the case for poetry-writing-as-living. She finds human truths by observing flowers and insects in the world around her. She seems to live by Keats's credo: "Poetry should come as easily as leaves to the trees, or else it had better not come at all." Collins conveys his poetic goal of close observation of the world around us by speaking as a writing teacher, mocking those readers and writers—*his* students?—who look for Great Symbolic Meaning in things (a mouse, a light switch) rather than valuing the things themselves.

I do not impose any formal requirements for the poem I ask students to write. I simply ask them to write a poem about poem writing. They can define poetry, respond to it, analyze themselves and their own writing. (Many students review their oeuvre, which is also a nice preparation for the book collections we work on next.)

Students often surprise me with their attitudes toward themselves and the creative process. Here are a few examples from my students:

The Last Poem

Writing poetry is
Finding the images
That stay
Because if you can just
Burn them
Long enough
Into someone's brain
They'll understand
What you felt
And that, my friend,
Is the real path
To world peace.

       —Jessica, grade 12

This poet has come to understand the importance of empathy in writing. She sees writers and readers engaged in an attempt to understand one another—and even sees writing as a source for world peace. This poem reminds me of Naomi Shihab Nye's book *Under This Same Sky,* the title of which comes from a poem that envisions world peace if only all people could come to understand that we share the same sky. I also like that Jessica refers to her audience as "my friend." This suggests a familiarity and a trust in her readers that grew as our course went on.

Poem

Poetry is the moment
                             When you slice a fresh watermelon
And the pink juice
          pours out
Making a puddle on the counter
And the icy flesh c o o l s
Your tongue
Before
You
Swallow
It
Whole.

—Nuala, grade 12

This poem is both powerful and sensual. I like the way the author lingers over the succulent details of the watermelon before the poem rushes to its conclusion. Her poem's presentation reinforces the subject of the poem itself.

Poetry Life

Don't try to be
                    Bly, Booth, Baraka
Don't try to be
          Hughes, Hopkins, Hall, or Haas
Don't try to be
          W.B., W.H., W.S., ee, or D.H.
Just be you.

—Andy, grade 12

This is a poem written by a student who just a couple of months earlier said he "never read poetry." This author dipped into a modern poetry anthology and surprised himself by finding strong preferences among the voices he heard there. Here, using the book's table of contents, he creates some fun patterns while passing on sound advice.

The Process

A monstrous, gushing volcano.
Wielding a heavy pick-axe
I approach its smoldering surface.

I strike the unyielding blue, kimberlite
And with each clank I widen the volcano's gash
Ever so slightly more.
If I'm lucky I will find a single rough, soot-covered rock,
Different from its brothers.
With a revolving paper-thin steel disc,
I cut off the ugly black dross
And place the rock inside an infernal oven
To burn away the last pieces of scum.
Then, into the night, I cleave and saw
Brute and girdle
Cut and slice
Like a murderous villain
Splitting the rock, against the grain,
And grind its lustrous surface
Into level, light-trapping facets.
When my butchering is done,
I stand amidst the rubble,
Gripping an untainted diamond,
The size of a baby pebble,
As pure as a newly completed poem.

—Charles, grade 12

This poem was written by a student who was terrified of poetry at the beginning of the term. He felt he wasn't creative enough and complained that it took him too long to write. (He often turned in assignments late.) But I never doubted his work ethic. I knew he wasn't being irresponsible. Instead, he had the great writerly instinct of wanting to revise his work until he was satisfied with it. The image of a murderous butcher relentlessly hacking away at the rock is one many writers may have envisioned upon receiving feedback from a demanding editor! This author seems to know that what Nabokov said about reading also holds true for writing: there is no such thing as writing, only rewriting.

Revision

One of the best reasons to work toward publication is that it makes the revision process real. When students are preparing manuscripts for publication, they are not working only to please their teacher; they are working to meet the demands of their readers in and out of the classroom. This also enables me to assume the role of coach. I am not the final arbiter of taste here. Rather, I am helping the student authors reach their desired audiences.

One way students revise their own work is through self-analysis. I ask them what they tried to accomplish in writing the poem and to mention any place they had trouble achieving their goals. They write these thoughts down on the back of their drafts so that my comments continue the dialogue they have begun.

I also have students read their poems out loud to the class. If they stumble over their own language, the language may be a problem. Then I have a different student read the poem out loud. This gives the author a chance to hear how the poem will be read by their audience. It is often revealing for authors to hear their poem read in a different way than they intended.

Aside from my comments and reading aloud, I remind students of the skills we have examined along the way. Together we list these skills, not as a collection of hard and fast rules to obey, but rather as a concrete inventory that forces students to reconsider their own work in a purposeful fashion. Or sometimes we trade poems in class and peer-edit one another's work by following these questions:

1. Where, if anywhere, is the language too general? (We began talking about specificity with our earliest writing exercises.)

2. Identify weak words (prepositions, articles, "to be" verbs). Are these words all necessary? Can you omit unnecessary language? (We discussed the importance of economical language in writing haiku.)

3. Do all the lines end in strong words? Where are line breaks most effective, most surprising? Where are they least effective, confusing? (We began talking about this idea with haiku as well and returned to it in all subsequent exercises.)

4. Verb check: Are all the verbs vivid? Can you picture the actions? If not, consider changing them.

5. Identify describing words (adjectives and adverbs). Are any of these words unnecessary? (For example, "dark red" might become "maroon.")

6. What are the most pleasing and most interesting sounds in the poem? Where, if anywhere, are the sounds distracting? (We talked about this with sound poems.)

7. Why does the poem have the number of stanzas it has? Why is the poem shaped the way it is? (We considered these issues particularly with the speed and sliding doors poems.)

8. Are there any places where the author uses repetition effectively? Any places where the repetition is merely redundant? (We discussed the power and the dangers of refrains when we discussed list poems.)

9. Where, if anywhere, were you confused while reading the poem? What might be added to clarify the poem?

10. How does the title of the poem prepare you for what follows?

Here are a couple of poems in first and later draft forms written after following these revision steps:

Flush (Draft 1)

The feel of the flush lever.
The whoosh of the flush itself.
The whirling wind of the water as
It circles into the wall of the toilet.

Sometimes the sound resembles that of
A sipping straw that has swallowed all but
the last drop.

Sometimes it resembles the crack at the break,
Of crashing wave, as it curls over the crest of
Its peak.

But it always has the same sound, that swallowing slurp at the
   end of its winding way.
That
Sound, I will never forget it.

—Spencer, grade 8

This poem was written in response to the sound assignment (see Chapter 7). While it features some interesting language in places, it is not yet very well shaped. Following the revision questions, we generated these responses (in bold):

1. Where, if anywhere, is the language too general? **This is not really the problem with this poem, but perhaps the final two lines "That / Sound, I will never forget."**

2. Identify weak words (prepositions, articles, "to be" verbs). Are these words all necessary? Can you omit unnecessary language? **Nearly every line has unnecessary language. "The feel" in line 1 is implied by the lever; the word "itself" in line 2; in line 5, the words "sometimes" and "resembles that of" seem unnecessary.**

3. Do all the lines end in strong words? Where are line breaks most effective, most surprising? Where are they least effective, confusing? **Lines 2–3, 5–6, 8, and 11 all end in weak words.**

4. Verb check: Are all the verbs vivid? Can you picture the actions? If not, consider changing them. **Some verbs are strong here (e.g., *circles*), but other verbs (*has, resembled*) are rather weak. By the way, see how *crack* in line 8 can replace *resembles* as the verb?** (I sometimes ask students to look for nearby nouns to take the place of weak verbs.)

5. Identify describing words (adjectives and adverbs). Are any of these words unnecessary? (For example, "dark red" might become "maroon.") **The word *flush* is unnecessary (It's the title!); the word *same* is already implied by *always*.**

6. What are the most pleasing and most interesting sounds in the poem? Where, if anywhere, are the sounds distracting? **There are some interesting sounds here—the "w" pattern in the first stanza; the "s" and "k" patterns below. These would become even more prominent if the poem were pruned of unnecessary language.**

7. Why does the poem have the number of stanzas it has? Why is the poem shaped the way it is? **The author said he had no reason for writing this poem as a four-stanza poem, and it's hard for me to see any advantage to writing it this way.**

8. Are there any places where the author uses repetition effectively? Any places where the repetition is merely redundant? **Some of the sound repetition is effective, but there are some redundancies I've already mentioned above.**

9. Where, if anywhere, were you confused while reading the poem? What might be added to clarify the poem? **It's not too confusing as it is.**

10. How does the title of the poem prepare you for what follows? **"Flush" just about says it all!**

Here is the author's final draft:

Flush (Final draft)

> The feel, the whoosh of the flush lever
> Whirling, winding water,
> Circling
> Into the toilet wall,
> The sound
> Like a sipping straw,
> Swallowing all
> but the last drop.

The crack at the break
                    A crashing wave,
                                  Curling
Over the crest
          Of its peak
                        Always the same

                             Swallowing

                             Slurp
                                At the end
                          Of its winding
                              Way.

This is not the most refined poem I've ever read, but the author did a wonderful job of revising his initial draft. His revision is significantly tighter and more interestingly presented than the initial draft.

Here is another poem that underwent many drafts. I include only the first and last drafts and a brief paragraph of the student's self-analysis:

The Gold Coin (Draft 1)

the woman faces ahead, the road passing under her
in the light of early morning.
her young son, behind her, rests his forehead
on the icy window.

the sun stood flat in the sky, dim morning mist
passing just in front of it.
the small boy lowers his window as much as it will go,
and the quick air streams through his hair.

now that the window is down, just below his eyes,
he soars over the lake, before the dim mist.

the boy looks at the gold coin fixed in the far distance,
so far that it seemed to move with the boy
through the thin mist and white sky.

gazing at the coin does not hurt his wide eyes,
its illuminated surface, like buttermilk, smooth,
but also hard.

it was made smooth from having journeyed
(the young boy imagined)
from the blackness at the bottom of the lake
and up through the heavy waters,

the vast fountain with no edges and without a bottom,
at the beginning of so many gone days.

the child reaches out and takes the sun,
turns it between his little fingers,
rubs its clean surface with his thumb.

—John, grade 12

This poem features some wonderfully interesting language, but it also reads as a rather obscure draft. Like W. C. Williams, who pruned his own rather short poem "Locust in Flower"—cutting it nearly in half "so he could see the tree"—this student cut about half of his lines and found a much clearer center: a central moment on an important journey. Even the new title signals a tighter command of the subject matter since the autumnal feeling pervades the entire poem.

Autumn Morning (Final draft)

my mother faced ahead. she drove along the lake,
the road humming, sweeping under us in the autumn morning.
i gazed at the lake, my small forehead on the icy glass,
behind the dry field browns and yellows of my mother's long
    hair.

i was the breeze, a quiet witness to the sky above the blue
    horizon,
above the restless berrywater of the lake, the blur under my
    eyes.
a spun mist drifted across the sky,
the soft strands of white lacing slowly.

the sun rested behind the morning mist,
the woolwhite over its face,
a small, round, pool of buttermilk,
a gold coin fixed high.

gazing at the sun did not strain my eyes that day.

The student offered this self-analysis:

> I think that my first draft of "Autumn Morning" is cluttered with too many details; the poem is written about my looking at the lake while my mother drove me to school one morning, and I think a poem describing such a smooth, relaxing hum of a car-ride and mesmerizing vastness of the lake should be told more simply and mysteriously. The experience placed me in a trance

in which a lot seemed to happen during a relatively brief time period, and I want the reader to experience this feeling too. So, I made it a point to shorten the poem, combining some details and expressing them in fewer words, implying much more than I say. For example, the words "berrywater" and "woolwhite" could have been extended into whole stanzas describing how the lakewater looked like thick, deep-colored juice from crushed berries and how the morning mist had the soft and hazy whiteness of wool, but this would have extended and tripped the pace of the poem. After my revising and condensing, I hope the overall effect is to have the reader left at the end feeling as if awoken from a slight daze in which more happened than would be expected with so short a poem.

Books of Poems

It is important for students, just as it is for professional writers, to have something to shoot for, culminating activities toward which they can be working and activities that can showcase everything they have learned in studying poetry. Publishing poetry is an excellent way to achieve these ends. I encourage students to submit their work to the school literary magazine. Beyond that, I encourage them to mail their work to reputable places that publish young authors and to enter local poetry contests. But these activities are beyond my control as a classroom teacher, and I want to ensure that every student has a successful experience publishing his or her own work. So I have students write their own books—class books and their own individual books of poetry. Both are useful in allowing students the opportunity to wrestle with the same problems professional writers face—revising, selecting, ordering, and introducing poems for publication.

Class Books

Class books are easy to create. I usually give students a set number of pages (say, three pages apiece) and have them choose poems to include. I have found it is better to require a set number of pages rather than a set number of poems in case some people's poems are much longer than others. I am always happy to help students choose poems—if they ask for help.

It is always interesting to see students struggle over which poems to include. They quickly understand that there is something reductive about a small sample of poems. (How can an author appear serious, smart, playful, funny, and deep in just a few pages?) It is also interesting to observe how students respond to the change in audience.

Every student in class will receive a copy of the book, not just the teacher, which means that people outside the walls of the classroom might read their work. For this reason, they may decide not to include certain poems, even poems you and the student think are their best work. But it is important to respect their privacy in these cases.

I solicit titles from the class, and we vote on a favorite book title from their suggestions. Publishing class books also allows students with special talents—in drawing a cover or in page layout—to excel. It is possible to produce high-quality books at fairly inexpensive prices at local copy centers, or even on school machines. Teachers and Writers Collaborative, a wonderful resource in New York City, also offers inexpensive production of poetry books in a unique online publication service.

Individual Books

I also ask students to create books of their own work. They include all the poems we have worked on thus far unless they have a special reason for not wanting to include certain poems. They need to select and arrange their work in a way that will be inviting and meaningful to their audience. I do not ask that these volumes be published in any fancy manner. Most students simply organize and photocopy their work by themselves, though even that responsibility raises interesting issues for writers. Should more than one poem appear on a page? What effect do blank pages have on the facing poems and on the book as a whole?

I do, however, insist on a couple of additional tasks in preparing these books. Students must review their earlier work and listen for patterns in their lives they have found themselves writing about. These choices are often not conscious, and many students are astonished at the thoughts that have dominated their writing over the course of the term. From this reflection, students must choose a title for their book, and they must write a short (typically one page) introduction to their readers. The introduction can offer autobiographical information about the author or prepare the reader for the poems to come. Some students use the introduction to share their self-reflections. Here are a couple of introductions my students have written:

Introduction to *Kid Stuff*

The title of this small anthology comes from my most frequent subject, my own childhood. Often, when I have trouble writing, I'll try to jog any old recollection and allow that to lead me to a piece's beginning, something concrete to start on. It not only revives the kinds of muscles that are most helpful when writing—

memory, focus, and imagination—but it is also a great way to give perspective to whatever identity you've shaped since then. Old Converse, baseball games, lemonade stands: putting these things on a page gives me an intimacy with those memories and space from them as well. I would say that most good poets share a lot of characteristics with the common kid. Surrounded by new things that excite us, we try to shed light on their meaning, making note of any detail that could help us shape a concept, and make sense of our world. If I could watch the world like a little kid watches it, I bet this poetry would come easy.

—Michael, grade 12

Introduction to *My Life*

Over the past two months we have written about everything from what was lying around a room to more personal objects and thoughts. We have even written while trying to be in the mindset of another person. Most of the things I've written are from a personal perspective, and revolve around my family and my past. What I have taken from this class is how to open up in words, and how to use styles to express different emotions.

This class has given me a new perspective on poetry. Through examining other poets' writing and trying to imitate that style and finding a style of our own. What I will take from this class is a new mindset on how to write and edit my own poems.

—Abby, grade 12

A Rather Lengthy Introduction to a Portfolio of Generally Brief Poetry

I am surprised by what I have learned and where my writing has gone this quarter. In addition to learning to write under strict deadlines (a new poem almost every day), I have gained a much sharper critical eye regarding my own work and a better intuition of how to revise and improve it. "Communication," for example, which I consider my best poem here, began shadily, and after an hour of ruthless picking became packed and virtually finished. This discriminating way of editing has also spilled over into the way I look at my prose; even in analytical papers I now look for how the language could be more poetically crafted to help the fluidity of the argument.

I also had not considered myself to be a great creative writer, but now I see that producing good creative writing can happen for pretty much anyone; it just takes some hard work to create the right impact. (I think writing good analytical stuff requires damning logical evidence; writing lasting creative stuff requires damning emotional substance and truth.) As I wrote more, I got a much better feel for poetry writing and my first drafts were better and contained less extraneous material from the outset. I became more aware of the need for strong images, as in haiku, and to make every word count. I am now a rabid fan of sensory detail, since that is the way we experience the world.

The most common subject in my poems is relationships, which is perhaps self-explanatory upon reading the poems. The majority of my poems are also depressing, or at least serious. (This seemed appropriate because I am not usually insightfully clever and witty and my attempts at comic writing are generally not as successful.) I also noticed an eerie pattern in these poems—they tended to juxtapose two images in order to increase the dramatic tension of the two competing forces pulling against one another. My poems were also rather short, but we should all be thankful for this after reading my endlessly verbose prose (think of my *Catcher in the Rye* paper!). In creative writing, at least, I tend to be a "less is more" fan. I usually find that the poem simply ends itself after two or three stanzas. Often my last stanza serves as the fulcrum, providing a second, antithetical image. After that there is nothing left to say.

—Jessica, grade 12

With the exercises described in this chapter, poetry writing in my classes has reached its culmination, but we have not ended our adventures in poetry writing. As William Stafford says in "Leaving a Writer's Conference": "Listen—if it was OK / this time, the world can surprise us / again." Just as students adopt different authorial personae in writing persona poems (see Chapter 8), they adopt a different persona in acknowledging their identity as poets, as the authors of books of poems. In so doing, they come to see their public (published) self as different from their private self.

In the final three chapters, we turn our attention to a new kind of wordplayground—performance. Performing poems offers not only another kind of public identity through the medium of one's own voice, but also an opportunity to reconsider everything students have thought about thus far: their writing and their identity.

10 Performance Tools: Punching, Pausing, Painting

A Life

Innocence?
In a sense.
In no sense!

Was that it?
Was that it?
Was that it?

That was it.

　　　　—Howard Nemerov

In this short poem, the speaker playfully assesses a life (his? the poet's? ours?) through puns, punctuation, and emphasis. The italics are not merely decorative; they also explicitly direct how the poem is to be read. Nemerov understands that how the words are spoken affects the meaning of the poem.

　　This chapter features a series of classroom exercises in preparation for performances outside the classroom (discussed in Chapters 11 and 12). Many of the exercises presented here follow up on ideas we began discussing while writing poems, and it is my hope that students ultimately consider performance not merely as an end in itself, but also as an important means by which they can become better readers and writers.

　　Here we pay close attention to words a reader might want to stress (or give more attention to), the speed of words (and the spaces in between words), and the way in which pronunciation can affect connotation. In other words, these exercises help students practice punching, pausing, and painting the words on the page.

Punching Words

All words are not created equal; some words are more important than others. This is clear in Nemerov's "A Life." His decision to italicize a different word in each line of stanza 2 makes the italicized word conspicuous, more important than it was in the other lines. It is also an invitation for the reader to say the italicized word louder in order to speak the graphic stress our eyes read on the page. Without the italics, we might read the lines flatly, as if each line were exactly the same. With the italics in place, the stresses are clearly marked, and the most important and interesting words get the attention they deserve.

Without this explicit direction, many of my students read flatly—not just in a monotone, but also without regard to emphasis. Yet most students are geniuses in hearing and speaking stresses in (sometimes very complicated) hallway conversations. Every student immediately knows that "I am not *going out* with her" does not mean "*I* am not going out with her." And that neither of these sentences remotely approaches the meaning of this one: "I am not going out with *her.*"

Because students are already expert at deciphering stress in ordinary conversations, I start with ordinary lines they might hear in their everyday lives before we consider lines from poems. I write a line on the board and underline a different word each time, having students take turns emphasizing a new word and explaining the connotative difference that results from the stress. This becomes part of our performance shorthand: underlined, or "punched," words announce words to be delivered with greater emphasis.

Take this line, for example: I really thought I knew her.

A. I really thought I knew her.
   (implies that I, for one, as opposed to, or unlike, anyone else)

B. I really thought I knew her.
   (implies that the knowledge was genuine and thorough, not casual)

C. I really thought I knew her.
   (emphasizes the past tense; she or he *once* though he knew her)

D. I really thought I knew her.
   (similar to first choice; a little more personal perhaps; the speaker feels betrayed)

E. I really thought I knew her.
   (not just a passing knowledge)

F. I really thought I knew her.
   (The speaker knew her better than he or she knew other people)

Other sentences that have worked well are these:

I'm really glad to see you here this evening.

Where did you get the money?

I don't want to sit there.

I often ask students to make up their own sentences (ones in which stressing a different word changes the subtext) and to present these to the class, explaining the connotative differences that result from stressing individual words.

Pausing

In poetry there are three general occasions to pause: (1) punctuation marks, (2) individual words within the poem, and (3) the position of words on the page—in particular, the way line breaks fall. (We considered pausing when we considered pacing in the sound and speed poems [see Chapter 7].)

Contrary to the belief of many of my students, *poets use punctuation*. What's more, they use it for the same reason all writers do—as a service to the reader. Punctuation helps the reader make sense of the language on the page and, in performance, guides the reader in delivering the lines.

I offer my students this brief review of punctuation devices:

Commas indicate brief pauses.

Pairs of commas indicate modifying and appositional material.

Dashes indicate longer pauses that tend to throw the action forward.

Colons indicate a movement from general to specific and suggest a still longer pause.

Semicolons separate independent clauses (dividing balanced items of equal weight) and separate complicated items within a list.

Periods indicate the end of sentences and require long, full stops.

In order to get students to attend to punctuation, I ask them to read an excerpt from Gertrude Stein's "She Bowed to Her Brother":

The story of how she bowed to her brother.
Who has whom as his.
Did she bow to her brother. When she saw him.
Any long story. Of how she bowed to her brother.
Sometimes not.
She bowed to her brother. Accidentally. When she
saw him.

Often as well. As not.
She did not. Bow to her brother. When she. Saw
him.

Here Stein's radical syntax and punctuation demand attention. Even as readers strain to race ahead, they are reined in by the abrupt full stops, which alter the meaning of the words. Consider how the sixth line would change if it read, "She bowed to her brother accidentally." The final word receives much more attention in the original. And this is part of Stein's point: how we read the story is, at least part of, the story.

Words within a poem can also suggest an occasion to pause. Consider a few examples: "Slowly I turn, step by step" or "I'm late, I'm late for a very important date." The connotations of the words that constitute these lines direct us to speak them slowly or quickly. Vowel sounds within individual words can also, more subtly, affect the speed of a line. Consider, for example, the final two lines of Frost's "Stopping by Woods on a Snowy Evening": "And miles to go before I sleep, / And miles to go before I sleep." Aside from the fact that the line is repeated, the lines are loaded with long vowel sounds (m**i**les, g**o**, **I,** sl**ee**p), which slow the reader down in imitation of the arduous journey the speaker describes.

Words that establish a pattern (like the repeated line in the last example) or break an established pattern also invite pauses. We might read the opening to Shelley's "Ode to the West Wind" ("O wild West Wind, . . .") with extra space between each word, enunciating clearly so that the *w*'s are not swallowed up. Or perhaps we would pause before the shift in the following poem written anonymously on a quotation board outside our student Writers' Center: "When you see my arm around someone else / when you see me smile goodbye / when I put you back on the shelf / **then** you'll know how I felt." Since *then* breaks the established pattern of lines beginning with *when,* we might pause before the last line to alert readers to the upcoming difference, particularly since it rhymes with the previous pattern.

Line breaks present another occasion to pause. Consider this poem by William Carlos Williams:

To a Poor Old Woman

munching a plum on
the street a paper bag
of them in her hand

They taste good to her.
They taste good

to her. They taste
good to her

You can see it by
the way she gives herself
to the one half
sucked out in her hand

Comforted
A solace of ripe plums
Seeming to fill the air
They taste good to her

The opening gesture of this poem, in which the title is part of the opening line, forecasts the playful syntax that follows. This is a challenging
poem to read because the line breaks are so unconventional. I want students to try to make sense of the syntax of these lines by themselves. A
reader might, for example, read through the first line break, pausing
after the word *street*. And we might treat the end of the first stanza as
the end of a sentence even though Williams offers no ending punctuation there.

The second stanza is especially interesting to read aloud. Williams
offers the same sentence broken three different ways. The first line is
end-stopped (that is, it ends a complete thought signified by the period).
But line 2 is enjambed (it is not syntactically concluded until the speaker
is midway through the third line). This effect changes not only the speed
at which the words are read, but also the significance of the words themselves. I ask students how the lines differ connotatively. They quickly
see that the end words receive more attention (just as we discussed in
writing haiku). As with the punching exercises, speakers of these words
might well say the end words louder (as if they were underlined or italicized). First we hear that the plums taste good *to her*; then that they *taste
good* (without regard to the old woman); and finally, that they even have
taste—a simple pleasure afforded to this "poor old woman."

Another poem that offers interesting line breaks and pacing is this
poem by Gwendolyn Brooks:

We Real Cool

> *The Pool Players.*
> *Seven at the Golden Shovel.*

We real cool. We
Left school. We

Lurk Late. We
Strike straight. We

Sing sin. We
Thin gin. We

Jazz June. We
Die soon.

This is, in fact, one of the first poems I ever heard performed as opposed to just read. Brooks practically sang this poem in readings, pausing extravagantly after each "we," as if to emphasize the herd mentality of the speaker who has no identity apart from his association with the larger group. The speaker is so willing to tie his identity to the group's identity that he even accepts "we'll die soon." Emphasizing the "we" in the first seven lines amplifies its absence in the last line.

In addition to punctuation marks that authors provide to guide readers' delivery of a poem, we use vertical lines in my classes to write in pauses we might want to emphasize in our readings. One vertical line indicates a short pause (equal to, say, a comma, for an unexpected twist on a word), and two vertical lines indicate long pauses (equal to a period, to provide extra dramatic attention to a word or moment within a poem). This notation serves as a reminder when reading the poem out loud, and it also offers a means by which one student can direct another to read the poem in a particular manner. We return to this idea in the next chapter.

Painting Words

The way words sound and the way they are pronounced can powerfully affect their connotations. This is why we can sometimes infer the emotional state or even the meaning of words spoken by a foreigner whose language we do not understand. Imbuing words with feeling—pronouncing words with sounds and emphases that imitate the meaning behind the words—is important in many everyday exchanges.

If, for example, someone invites you to a party by saying, "It'll be fun," your response may well be guided by the way they say the word *fun*. If the word is spoken flatly, you might take their offer as perfunctory; if the word is spoken with excitement (yes, in a "fun" way), you'll likely receive the offer more warmly.

Or consider the example of radio advertising. In a thirty-second spot without pictures, the advertiser tries to sell listeners a product, service, or idea through words, by the way words are "painted," or expressed. In class, I write two popular radio slogans on the board:

> "Nothing but mellow songs to soothe you through the night. Light favorites."
>
> "Rockin' hard all night long. The Drive."

I ask students to single out words that could be painted. We might, for example, pronounce "mellow, soothe, light" in a mellow, smooth, light voice. By contrast, fans of hard rock might soon be lost if we softened "rockin'" or "drive." Students immediately seize key words and imitate the DJ voices they have heard many times.

Here are some sample sentences students might practice with before we look at poems:

1. Sweet Baby Ray's fiery hot sauce will set your meal ablaze.
2. The sand was soft and warm, and the surf rolled in gently.
3. She spilled a huge gallon-sized jug of Kool-Aid right on my new suede jacket. I felt sticky and gross all day long.
4. That sweet little old lady from down the street came over with a plate of sugar cookies that were still warm.
5. My boss is so cuckoo he spits when he talks and screams like an ape even if you're just five or ten minutes late.
6. The mountain we call, in whispers, *Catalina*.
7. My face is soft, opal, a feathering of snow against the cold black leather coat which is night.
8. We lie down screaming as rain punches through.
9. Spray-painted offerings on walls offer a chaos of colors.
10. This concrete river becomes a steaming, bubbling snake of water, pouring over nightmares of wakefulness, pouring out a rush of birds, a flow of clear liquid on a cloudless day.

(The last five entries are lines taken from poems by Diane Wakoski, Rita Dove, and Luis Rodriguez. I like to mix in lines from poems and even pop songs to underscore the idea that our performance painting is not a practice limited to performance poetry.)

When I give this list to students, I ask them to circle words they plan to color. They are often able to see right away that the words they circle are strong words (like the strong end words we talked about in relation to haiku). Circling painted words completes our performance shorthand.

It's also possible to color the same word in different ways. Consider the song "I Love You" as performed by Frank Sinatra. As a line reader, Sinatra has few equals. Many fellow singers talked about his inventive choices and his ability to sell listeners on the personae he creates. Although the title recurs many times throughout the song, Sinatra never says the line exactly the same way—not even when he says, "The same old words I'm saying in the same old way." As a class, we try to identify the moods and feelings embedded in his readings.

I write the sentence "I love you" on the board and ask students to imagine all the different possible readings for these three words. Students not only invent different readings, but they actually tell stories about these "characters" as well. Just as we discussed in writing persona poems (see Chapter 8), students hear how different personae are created by different readings of the same lines.

One student, for example, said, "Okay, she's saying 'I love you,' but she's just trying not to hurt his feelings. She's already planning to break up with him a couple of weeks from now." I allow students to generate any story they want—even incredibly difficult performance challenges like this one—provided they take a shot at performing that scene. As a class, we can then discuss how successfully the intended effects were achieved.

To spur discussion, or to pursue finer distinctions, I ask for volunteers: How would you say "I love you" to someone you loved? How would a boy say it to his mother on Mother's Day and how would this differ from the way he'd say it to his father on Father's Day? What we're really getting at here is persona; students imagine not only different stresses but also the *kinds* of people, the situations, that would occasion such readings. The development of personae continues to be a focus of the performance activities explored in the following section, Performing Children's Poems, as well as in the activities of performing poems from canonical literature and from students' own original poems, discussed in the following chapters.

Performing Children's Poems

Reading to my children at home always reminds me how much fun it can be to read aloud. This is a big part of why I always start performance work in my classes using children's poems. Many children's poems are meant to be hammed up. There is also something wonderfully liberating about working with children's literature. First, the words and the meanings are easy, so everyone can perform their lines well. Second, there is no "sacred text" burden here as there is when reading from Shakespeare or Wordsworth, so we can just concentrate on having fun with language.

We start with a poem from a picture book I read to my own children.

Quick as a Cricket

I'm as quick as a cricket.
I'm as slow as a snail.
I'm as cold as a toad.
I'm as hot as a fox.
I'm as weak as a kitten.
I'm as strong as an ox.
I'm as loud as a lion.
I'm as quiet as a clam.
I'm as tough as a rhino.
I'm as gentle as a lamb.
I'm as brave as a tiger.
I'm as shy as a shrimp.
I'm as happy as a lark.
I'm as nice as a bunny.
I'm as mean as a shark.
I'm as tame as a poodle.
I'm as wild as a chimp.
I'm as lazy as a lizard.
I'm as small as an ant.
I'm as large as a whale.
I'm as sad as a basset.
I'm as busy as a bee.
Put it all together, and you've got me.

—Audrey Wood

This poem from a picture book is particularly fun for students to read. It not only resembles the "I am . . ." poems they wrote earlier in the term (see Chapter 4), but it also beautifully reinforces the punching, pausing, and painting exercises we've just worked on.

This poem has twenty-three lines, so it might roughly match the number of students in a classroom, giving each student one line. (If you have more students, you could appoint students who aren't reading to be directors, who comment on the choices the performers make. The poem is also so short that it's easy to do a second or third reading to get everyone involved.)

This activity practically works by itself. Even without reminders, students instinctively do interesting things with their lines—buzzing the *s* in *busy*, adopting a cheesy French accent for the "poodle" line. It's true that some students are still tentative. My process here is the same one I follow when students read their poems aloud: no one may comment until the poem is finished. We applaud the reading, compliment the choices we think are most effective, and only then suggest other choices the reader might have made. If a student said the "loud as a lion" line in a soft, timid voice, for example, we would suggest the speaker try it again, this time shouting the line.

Aside from all the other advantages, children's poetry provides performers with ready audiences. I was lucky to teach at an N (nursery)–12 school with lots of young children (read: lots of potential audiences) right down the hall. But at any high school there may be young audiences nearby who would love to attend a performance. This is a very Deweyan notion: students are doing the work of actors, and not merely performing for one another within the classroom, but performing for actual audiences other than themselves, making the life of the school resemble life outside of the school.

We follow up this performance activity with another children's poem, this one from Dr. Seuss:

My Many Colored Days

Some days are yellow.

Some are blue.
On different days
I'm *different* too.

You'd be surprised how many ways

I change on *different* colored days.

On bright red days how good it feels to be a horse
And kick my heels!

On other days I'm other things.
On bright blue days
I flap my wings.

Some days, of course,
Feel sort of brown,

Then I feel slow and low,
Low
  Down.

Then comes a yellow day.
And I am a busy, buzzy bee.

Gray day . . . everything is gray.
I watch. But nothing moves today.

Then all of a sudden
I'm a circus seal!
On my orange days that's how I feel.

Green days. Deep deep in the sea.
Cool and quiet fish. That's me.

On purple days I'm sad.
I groan. I drag my tail.
I walk alone.

But when my days are happy pink,
It's great to jump
And just not think.

Then come my black days
Mad and loud. I howl,
I growl at every cloud.

Then comes a mixed-up day
And what! I don't know who
Or what I am.

But it all turns out all right, you see.
And I go back to being me.

After an initial reading in which each student takes a line, I ask them to consider how they can punch, pause, and paint the words in these lines. I want students to suggest the extra slow reading of the "brown" line, just as I want them to hear the difference between "blue" and "bright blue" and to play with patterns in the language (exaggerating the string of long *e* sounds in the "green" entry, for example). Even on relatively ordinary lines (e.g., "You'd be surprised how many ways"), they need to decide which word(s) to punch and how to say the word *surprised* in a surprised voice.

This poem is not only easy to read, but it also adds a performance element: gesture. Students "kick their heels" and "flap their wings," which the lines direct readers to do. We consider other lines in which nothing is explicitly suggested and think of ways to physicalize the words (How would a bee move? How does a circus seal act?).

The promise of an audience does wonders. My students eagerly debated readings and gestures that might most appeal to younger children. One student suggested we wear colors that matched our individual lines; another suggested face paint. In a single class period, my students were ready to consider this poem a theater piece.

Another children's poem I've used is "The Maestro Plays," a funny piece featuring playful adverbs that are easy to ham up in reading. This poem appears in a picture book with wonderfully vivid illustrations, but I don't show my students these pictures since the images might overdetermine the range of vocal and physical choices the readers make.

The Maestro Plays

The maestro plays.
He plays proudly.
He plays loudly.

He plays slowly
He plays oh-ly.

He plays reachingly.

He plays beseechingly.

He plays flowingly
Glowingly . . .
Knowingly . . .
Showingly . . .
Goingly . . .

Now he is playing singingly.

He is playing ringingly, wingingly . . .
Swingingly, flingingly, tingingly, faster, faster . . .

He plays busily.
He plays dizzily.

He stops. He mops his brow.

The maestro begins
Playing again mildly . . .

But suddenly he's playing wildly . . .
He bows furiously
He jabs!
He stabs!
He saws!
He slaps the strings.

He plays trrrr-r-r-r-ippingly.

He plays skippingly . . .

—Bill Martin Jr.

Teachers have many wonderful children's poems to choose from. I have found librarians, colleagues, parents, and my students themselves to be great resources for additional poems. The range of children's literature is so great that it is also easy to accommodate the interests of a prospective audience. One of the first times my classes performed poems was before an audience of first and second graders who were studying insects. This topic gave us focus, and we decided to perform choral poems about insects.

Choral Poems

Paul Fleischman's *Joyful Noise,* a Newbery Award–winning book of children's choral poems about insects, is meant to be read aloud, to be performed. What's different about these poems is that they are written for two voices: each poem features two columns, one for each reader. Here is a sample from a poem called "Grasshoppers":

Speaker A	Speaker B
Grasshoppers	Grasshoppers
hopping	hopping
high	
Grasshoppers	Grasshoppers
jumping	jumping
Valuting from	
leaf to stem	
stem to stem	leaf to leaf
plant to plant	stem to stem
	Grass—
leapers	leapers
Grass—	
bounders	bounders
	Grass—
springers	springers . . .

Both speakers read the first two lines simultaneously. But line 3 is spoken only by speaker A. Speaker B has a rest on line 3, the same way a violinist in an orchestra might have a rest during a passage of music. In line 8, the two speakers are reading different words at the same time, creating a sort of verbal harmony.

I take advantage of every opportunity to compare poem readings to music. Our shorthand notation (underlining punched words, using vertical lines for pauses, and circling painted words) is tantamount to scoring a poem, the same way a musician scores a piece of music. And many of the activities in the following chapters relate poetry reading to music.

Joyful Noise consists of fourteen poems, and because students need to perform these poems in pairs (or threes or fours), this set of poems easily accommodates an entire class. Teachers looking for a different subject might be interested in another of Fleischman's books of choral poems, *I Am Phoenix,* which features poems of the same genre, all written about birds.

To accommodate the needs of other audiences, or to remind students of the connection between writing and performance, I sometimes ask students to write their own choral poems. Here's a choral poem two middle school students wrote for a primary school class that was working on an "ocean" unit:

Squids

I am a squid	I am a squid
a misunderstood	creature
	given
by sailors a	
	bloodthirsty feature.
I am a squid	I am a squid
loaded with suckers	
	to catch all the fish that are
just out of luckers.	out of luckers.
I am a squid	I am a squid
armed with	
	black ink
for in order to escape	
	I often must sink.
I am a squid.	I am a squid
with	
two	two
hungry arms	
	that do to my prey
a great deal of harm.	
I am a squid	I am a squid
with 8 legs and arms	
	that dart through the sea
to catch food	
	for
ME!	ME!

—Sheridan and BJ, grade 7

These two poets researched their subjects (as discussed in Chapter 8), and they include some interesting facts in their funny and light presentation. They never speak different words at the same time, but they alternate lines nicely, paying attention to line breaks and using each other as the straight man for the punch lines they deliver. The squid performers also gamely adopted a performance persona here, wearing face paint and tentacles made from pipe cleaners.

The Fleischman choral poems and the ones the students write themselves are fun to rehearse and easy to read. Also, through the initial rehearsal, students are working with only one other student, thus drastically reducing their performance anxiety. I walk around the room and encourage them to both support and challenge each other: What gestures could you use to support these lines? How can you paint the word *fear* or the word *joy* more clearly? How can you make sure you are both heard in that final line?

These early performances are always positive. Young children love the guest-star appearances, and their teachers appreciate the change of pace and the connection of poetry to whatever they are studying. Very young students often idolize older students. Even the most insecure, nervous students seem "cool" and "glamorous" to the primary school audience. My students were once asked for their autographs by a nursery school audience!

This chapter explores how students can begin to consider different ways of reading aloud—punching, pausing, and painting words. While we all use these tools in our everyday lives, I want students to become more conscious of the effect these devices have on their readers and listeners. Additionally, these performance exercises reinforce the writing exercises we've done: students are better able to see the effects their stylistic choices have on readers.

These early performance exercises help students establish some concrete performance terms and a concrete system of notation for these terms (underlining words to punch, writing vertical lines to mark pauses, and circling words to paint with their voices). They also begin exploring the idea of a dramatic persona. We continue to develop all of these skills and ideas when we look at performing more complicated poems and begin examining the dramatic personae of our own speakers (see Chapter 11).

11 Performance: Stage Persona

All the world's a stage,
And all the men and women merely players;
They have their exits and their entrances,
And one man in his time plays many parts.

William Shakespeare, from *As You Like It* (2.3.139–42)

In this speech, Shakespeare suggests that all of life is a series of performances. In our everyday lives, we play a variety of roles—teacher, student, administrator, parent, child—and we make complex blocking, costuming, and scripting decisions every day in how we act, in what we wear, and in what we say. These choices announce who we are, or at least the kind of person we would like others to think of us as.

In fact, the word *person* comes from the word *persona*. The etymology goes back to Greek theater, in which actors wore masks to convey the identity of the character they were playing. While we don't wear literal masks except on Halloween or at costume parties, we often mask our feelings, our politics, our ideas, our values. The degree to which we advertise or conceal ourselves also says something about who we are.

Notions of identity are very important to my students. Adolescence, roughly the period between the ages of twelve and eighteen, is, according to developmental psychologist Erik Erikson, centered on the idea of identity formation. Adolescents, according to Erikson, are consumed by the desire to answer a single question, "Who am I?"

My students have already adopted different personae—spoken in different voices—in their persona poems (see Chapter 8). And they experiment nearly every day with ways to present themselves and with how they would like to be seen. I'm thinking now of the perfectionist girl who dyed her hair purple last year; the boy with three different blinding white warm-up suits, daring someone to sully them; the boy with multiple piercings who has begun experimenting with makeup; the girl with close-cropped hair who wrote "I'm not a guy" in permanent marker on her clothes. As Oscar Wilde said, "The first duty in life is to assume a pose. What the second duty is, no one has yet discovered." The study of personae is not only useful in helping students understand their emerging identities, but also a topic of great interest and relevance to their lives.

In this chapter, I present exercises that help students study the personae of a variety of different speakers and consider ways of conveying these personae through performance. We work as a whole class initially. Then I ask students to work together in small groups to present speakers to the class. These steps prepare students to try solo performances of poems other people have written and of poems they have written themselves.

Class Example: Discovering Persona

As a starting point, we use William Stafford's "Fifteen," a poem about a teenage boy who witnesses a motorcycle crash that changes forever who he is and how he sees the world:

Fifteen

South of the bridge on Seventeenth
I found back of the willows one summer
day a motorcycle with engine running
as it lay on its side, ticking over
slowly in the high grass. I was fifteen.

I admired all that pulsing gleam, the
shiny flanks, the demure headlights
fringed where it lay; I led it gently
to the road, and stood with that
companion, ready and friendly. I was fifteen.

We could find the end of a road, meet
the sky out on Seventeenth. I thought about
hills, and patting the handle got back a
confident opinion. On the bridge we indulged
a forward feeling, a tremble. I was fifteen.

Thinking, back farther in the grass I found
the owner, just coming to, where he had flipped
over the rail. He had blood on his hand, was pale—
I helped him walk to his machine. He ran his hand
over it, called me good man, roared away.

I stood there, fifteen.

—William Stafford

I read the poem aloud to the class and then split up the class into groups. Together they answer the same set of questions we examined when we wrote persona poems (see Chapter 8). Then I re-form the class and we compare answers. Here is a sample of the kinds of responses (in bold) one class came up with:

1. Is the speaker a man or a woman? **A boy on the verge of manhood.**

2. How old is she or he? **Fifteen!**

3. How early does the person wake up? **Early; he sounds adventurous.**

4. What would this person eat for breakfast? **A big meal. He wanders far away, and he's a growing boy.**

5. What kind of family life does this person have? Does she or he live alone or with relatives? **Not clear from the poem. No one from his family is identified. But this stranger is a kind of father figure for the boy. He confers upon him the title "good man" in the final stanza.**

6. What kind of clothes does the person wear? **Nothing fancy, blue jeans.**

7. What kind of job does the person hold? **He has no job. Right now he seems to be free, wandering around trying things out.**

8. What kind of car does the person drive? **He doesn't drive. That's part of his fascination with the motorbike. Driving will allow him to go farther away from home, travel and learn more.**

9. What kind of music does the person listen to? **"Wild Thing." He wants to be daring and wild.**

10. How many friends does this person have? **Not many. He sees the motorcycle as a "companion," a friend he can go on all sorts of wild adventures with.**

11. How wealthy is this person? **Not wealthy. He seems to be from a small town. He's awed by a motorcycle.**

12. How well educated is this person? **Don't know. He does use fancy words like "demure."**

13. What would the person's favorite subject in school be? **Driver's ed.? This kid is dying to bust out of his little world.**

14. What kind of book would this person read? *On the Road.*

15. What is this person's favorite movie? *Independence Day* **or maybe** *Thunder Road.*

16. What is this person's greatest dream or aspiration? **He wants to be his own person, be his own man. He's tired of being treated like a kid.**

17. Name a turning point in the person's life and explain how it

has changed him or her. How has it changed the way you see him or her? **This guy saw a bike crash and it left him wanting to leave his own life behind. Even though it's scary, he knows he's in the real world now, and he wants to break free from all the rules children face.**

Although the students' answers obviously don't discuss every aspect of the poem, they do get to the poem's central issue—the narrator's coming-of-age. I have added a new final question here about turning points as a way of introducing what John Ciardi and Miller Williams call the "fulcrum" of a poem, the point on which the poem turns. From the time we considered two-word poems and the resonance between words, ideas, images, or stories (Chapter 3), we've tacitly considered fulcrums. Here, I'm introducing it more formally since, as Charlotte Lee and Timothy Gura argue in *Oral Interpretation*, it's a very useful tool in preparing poems for performance.

Ciardi and Williams say fulcrums are usually found within the poem but that they can occur after the final line. One class debated the location of the fulcrum in this very poem. Some argued that the final stanza signals a change (the speaker is called a "man," and they note that the final sentence is different from the ending sentence in the three previous stanzas). Another group saw the poem as a nostalgic look back by a much older, wiser narrator ("I *was* fifteen"). A third group saw the fulcrum as coming after the poem ends. They envisioned the narrator planning to throw himself headlong into the world of adulthood as the poem ends. In other words, they saw very little time elapsing between the crash and his reporting of the event. All of these are possible readings of the poem, I tell them, but I insist that students take a definite stance of some sort before performing the poem. They have to have a clear reading in mind that they hope to convey to their audience.

But, having decided on a reading, how can a performer convey these thoughts to an audience through a single reading of the poem? Here we return to our punch, pause, and paint exercises (Chapter 10). I ask students to make five punch, pause, and paint choices in total. (They are always welcome to make more.) Then they justify those choices in front of the class. Here is a "score" of the poem as one class saw it. Remember, "punched" words are underlined, pauses are indicated by vertical lines, and "painted" words are circled.

Fifteen

South of the <u>bridge</u> | on <u>Seventeenth</u> |
I found back of the willows one summer

day a motorcycle with engine running
as it lay on its side, (ticking) over
slowly in the high grass. I was fifteen.

I admired all that (pulsing) gleam, the
shiny flanks, the (demure) headlights
fringed where it lay; I led it gently
to the road, and stood with that
<u>companion</u>, | ready and (friendly) I was fifteen.

We could find the end of a road, meet
the | sky | on out Seventeenth. I thought about
hills, and patting the handle got back a
confident opinion. On the bridge we indulged
a forward feeling, a tremble. I <u>was</u> fifteen.

Thinking, back farther in the grass I found
the owner, just coming to, where he had flipped
over the rail. He had blood on his hand, was pale—
I helped him walk to his machine. He ran his hand
over it, called me good man, (roared) away.

→   →

I stood there, fifteen.

Notice that they've punched the word *bridge* to mark the narrator's transition; the word *Seventeenth*, the number just before the majority age; the word *companion*, personifying the motorcycle; the word *end*, to signify the end of the narrator's childhood; and the word *was* in the last line, to emphasize the past tense—the narrator has become a man. (This last choice reminds me of the exercise in Chapter 10 of reading William Carlos Williams's lines containing the same words emphasized in different ways.)

The performers have built in a pause before and after "on Seventeenth" to dramatize the boundary line the narrator is crossing; a longer pause than usual after the word *companion*—maybe the narrator is trying out this word, this new identity he is forging; a pause around the word *sky*, because some listeners were hearing this line as "meet this guy"; very short pauses in the penultimate sentence—it's all coming to a quick end for the narrator. I like that these students have chosen to draw arrows to signal the de-emphasized punctuation stops. Students should feel free to use any new notation marks that aid them in their performance of the poem.

They have chosen to paint the words *ticking* (exaggerating the clock noises embedded within the word); *pulsing* (exploding the first syllable to reveal the throbbing excitement of the narrator); *demure* (said in a soft, shy voice); *friendly* (said in a cheerful, smiling way); and *roared* (said in a rough, growling voice, demonstrating the power of the machine and the power the boy craves).

After each reading, we follow the same procedure we use after poem writing exercises. That is, we applaud the reading and point out effective choices. Only then do I solicit ways of making the performance stronger. I ask, "Where, if anywhere, were you confused? What other choices might the reader have made here?" I never accept vague answers (e.g., "I just didn't like it," or "The whole thing had no energy"); I insist that the audience point out specific questions or suggestions ("Why did you stress the word *motorcycle*?"; "Why wouldn't you pause after the word *blood*?") Performers get immediate feedback after each performance, and they can always try again if there's time.

Next, just as we did with children's poems, we think about ways of physicalizing choices. These come out right away with practice readings. Should this performer slouch, or swagger? Should his posture ever change? Here again, the idea of the fulcrum is useful. "Where is the fulcrum in the poem?" I ask, and "How can body language convey the turning point?"

Should the performer try to imitate any of the words with hand gestures (e.g., pointing to the "sky," "patting the handle" of the motorcycle)? Classroom audiences are quick to praise such gestures—and quick to eliminate them if they seem too heavy-handed. One class silently acted out the "dramatic narrative" of the poem—the fallen biker being led to his motorcycle by the narrator—while the rest of the class performed the poem chorally.

Another possibility is to add sound or music to the performance of the poem. With this group, some wanted to add the "vroom, vroom" noise at the end (like the introduction to the song "Leader of the Pack," I thought); others wanted a kind of ominous bass line beneath the reading of the poem to signal the drama of the moment. I never eliminate choices out of hand. I much prefer to have students try them out and see how well they work in performance. (I offer more poem-music possibilities in the next chapter.)

Group Performances of First-Person Poems

Now we're ready to review the steps we've used to prepare a poem for performance:

1. What is the narrator's attitude toward the subject?

2. Where is the fulcrum of the poem?

3. What punch, pause, and paint choices would help to clarify the narrator's attitude toward the audience?

4. What gestures might help bring the poem alive?

5. Would music or sound accompaniment make the performance stronger?

I divide the class into small groups of four to five and give students these poems: Sonnet 29 by Shakespeare; "To His Coy Mistress" by Andrew Marvell; "Nikki-Rosa" by Nikki Giovanni; and "since feeling is first" by e. e. cummings. I tell each group they need to perform their poem *as a group,* making sure everyone gets involved. Furthermore, I insist that each group provide at least one symbolic prop or costume. Then I encourage them to follow the same steps we have just reviewed and give them a class period to prepare a performance of the poem for the entire class.

Sonnet 29

When in disgrace with Fortune and men's eyes,
I all alone beweep my outcast state,
And trouble deaf heaven with my bootless cries,
And look upon myself and curse my fate,
Wishing me like to one more rich in hope,
Featur'd like him, like him with friends possess'd,
Desiring this man's art, and that man's scope,
With what I most enjoy contented least;
Yet in these thoughts myself almost despising,
Haply I think on thee—and then my state,
(Like to the lark at break of day arising
From sullen earth) sings hymns at heaven's gate;
  For thy sweet love remembered such wealth brings
  That then I scorn to change my state with kings.

Shakespearean sonnets work very well because they usually have an unmistakable turning point. Sonnet 29 offers such a turning point. In the first eight lines, the narrator laments his lack of worldly riches and influence, but the word *yet* that opens line 9 signals a turning point. The speaker realizes that his beloved offers him incomparably greater riches.

A Shakespearean actor associated with the Folger Institute once suggested the performance activity of having each member of a group say a line. The first member lies down "in disgrace" with his face covered; by lines 5 and 6, actors might be sitting up and gesturing to the people the narrator envies, "like him . . . like him"; by the turning point, the group rises. The narrator is clearly standing tall by the end of the poem.

I have used this exercise as is, and I am happy to share it with any group of performers who are stuck. On the other hand, I don't want to infringe on their creativity, so I simply ask the group if they'll be sitting or standing when they read this poem. To my astonishment, one group nearly duplicated the Folger exercise by themselves. This group's props were literal but effective. The early speakers pointed to people wearing fancy watches or jewelry, and the last speaker threw away monopoly money when the narrator realizes his beloved is worth more than mere money.

To His Coy Mistress

> Had we but world enough, and time,
> This coyness, lady, were no crime.
> We would sit down and think which way
> To walk, and pass our long love's day.
> Thou by the Indian Ganges' side
> Should'st rubies find; I by the tide
> Of Humber would complain. I would
> Love you ten years before the Flood,
> And you should, if you please, refuse
> Till the conversion of the Jews.
> My vegetable love should grow
> Vaster than empires, and more slow.
> An hundred years should go to praise
> Thine eyes, and on thy forehead gaze:
> Two hundred to adore each breast,
> But thirty thousand to the rest;
> An age at least to every part,
> And the last age should show your heart.
> For, lady, you deserve this state,
> Nor would I love at lower rate.
> But at my back I always hear
> Time's winged chariot hurrying near;
> And yonder all before us lie
> Deserts of vast eternity.
> Thy beauty shall no more be found;
> Nor, in thy marble vault, shall sound

My echoing song; then worms shall try
That long-preserved virginity,
And your quaint honour turn to dust,
And into ashes all my lust.
The grave's a fine and private place,
But, none, I think, do there embrace.
   Now therefore, while the youthful hue
Sits on thy skin like morning dew,
And while thy willing soul transpires
At every pore with instant fires,
Now let us sport us while we may;
And now, like amorous birds of prey,
Rather at once our time devour,
Than languish in his slow-chapped power.
Let us roll all our strength and all
Our sweetness, up into one ball,
And tear our pleasures with rough strife
Thorough the iron gates of life.
Thus, though we cannot make our sun
Stand still, yet we will make him run.

"To His Coy Mistress" is a much longer poem but also a fun one to perform. The narrative—the narrator uses the rhetorical ploy of reminding his beloved of her mortality in order to seduce her into action in the present—is clear even to students who complain that the language is "too old-fashioned." What is also nice about this poem is the obvious break in the middle. Line 21 not only opens with the word *but* that sets up the contrast to come, but it is also indented.

One group that took on this poem broke it into four sections (lines 1–10, 11–20, 21–32, and 33–46), one for each member of the group. They had fun punching and painting the evocative language. They later told me that "pausing is the most important aspect of this poem. It starts off slow because he's mocking this girl who thinks she has all the time in the world. But then he races faster when he gets impatient and he's laying it on thick."

This group also had fun with props. The third speaker, who began to race faster, got dressed up like Flavor Flav from Public Enemy, complete with baseball cap akilter and a gigantic clock around his neck. His costume screamed, "Time is running out!" This third speaker also approached the seated beloved from a different direction, as if to suggest he was trying a new tack.

The Nikki Giovanni and the e. e. cummings poems are much more difficult to perform, even though they are much more modern. (I assigned them to kids who had already done theater training.) What makes them especially challenging is the absence of punctuation. It is more difficult to divide these poems into neat parts. Even the beginnings and endings of lines are ambiguous. But the attitudes—proud and resentful in the first case and head over heels in love in the second—are clear.

Nikki-Rosa

childhood remembrances are always a drag
if you're Black
you always remember things like living in Woodlawn
with no inside toilet
and if you become famous or something
they never talk about how happy you were to have
your mother
all to yourself and
how good the water felt when you got your bath
from one of those
big tubs that folk in Chicago barbecue in
and somehow when you talk about home
it never gets across how much you
understood their feelings
as the whole family attended meetings about Hollydale
and even though you remember
your biographers never understand
your father's pain as he sells his stock
and another dream goes
and though you're poor it isn't poverty that
concerns you
and though they fought a lot
it isn't your father's drinking that makes any difference
but only that everybody is together and you
and your sister have happy birthdays and very good
Christmasses
and I really hope no white person ever has cause
to write about me
because they never understand
Black love is Black wealth and they'll
probably talk about my hard childhood

and never understand that
all the while I was quite happy.

since feeling is first
who pays any attention
to the syntax of things
will never wholly kiss you;

wholly to be a fool
while Spring is in the world

my blood approves,
and kisses are a better fate
than wisdom
lady I swear by all flowers. Don't cry
—the best gesture of my brain is less than
your eyelids' flutter which says

we are for each other:then
laugh, leaning back in my arms
for life's not a paragraph

And death i think is no parenthesis

The "Nikki-Rosa" group featured a circle of confused reporters (the "biographers" Giovanni's narrator mentions) surrounding the speakers, literally taking note of the things the narrator says are usually ignored "if you're Black." In this way, the group showed how Giovanni's poem itself is helping to conquer the condition the narrator laments. The cummings group featured an actor plucking flower petals during the entire reading, slowly and deliberately mouthing, "She loves me. She loves me. She loves me."

In performing these poems—these new personae—for the class, students learn how to convey language through costuming, blocking, and props. They invent them on their own and they learn from one another. The next step is for students to perform before audiences outside of the classroom. In the next chapter, we consider other wordplaygrounds to explore—performances with other classes and other disciplines, readings in libraries and coffeehouses, and poetry projects with other schools.

12 Performance: Beyond the Boundaries

Although it is not yet evening,
The secretaries have changed their frocks
As if it were time for dancing,
And locked up in the scholars' books
There is a kind of rejoicing
There is a kind of singing.

—Howard Moss, from "The Persistence of Song"

This poem reminds us of the ways in which many of us compartmentalize our lives. We arrange our lives in discrete units: there is a time for reading, a time for working, and a time for dancing, and they all remain separate from one another. But these units are artificial, of course, and they can be very confusing. Schools offer some of the most rigid and confusing compartments of all. Rushing from class to class, students must shift their focus from math to English to music to chemistry with no apparent connection between these different spheres of study (to say nothing of their home lives and social lives, which constantly vie for attention). As Maxine Greene argues, "Surely at least part of the challenge [of teaching] is to refuse artificial separations of the school from the surrounding environment, to refuse the decontextualizations that falsify so much" (11).

In this chapter, I challenge some of the assumptions that go along with this compartmentalization: Why is rejoicing locked up in books? Why can't schools offer a place for rejoicing? Why do we maintain rigid distinctions between disciplines? Why can't poems, for example, be seen through other media—music, art, dancing, theater? Why do students often see so little connection between their lives in and out of school? Poetry can provide such a connection. I consider new ways to perform poems and new wordplaygrounds on which to perform them. Specifically, I present poetry exercises that go beyond the artificial walls of academic disciplines and then suggest ways of organizing public performances that take students beyond the walls of the school as well.

Poetry and Music

Combining poetry and music in the classroom has always been a natural connection for me. The lexicon of poetry is filled with musical terms:

rhythm, sound, tone, resonance, meter. As mentioned in an earlier chapter, I have even suggested that my students prepare to read poems aloud by considering the poem as a musical score. But, more than that, music is already a big part of most of my students' lives. Many of my students play instruments and the vast majority listen to several hours of music each day. I want to take advantage of their interest and their expertise.

I use poetry and music together chiefly in two ways. The first is by beginning class each day with a reading accompanied by a recording. This is a great ritual introduction to each class and so short—it takes about five minutes—that it leaves plenty of time for other reading, writing, and performing activities.

In my own music listening life, I have always liked the idea of blending spoken word and musical recordings. Perhaps the first time I was aware of this was listening to Simon and Garfunkel's "Seven o'Clock News/Silent Night." While a sweet and standard rendition of the Christmas song "Silent Night" is playing, a newscaster's voice rattles off disturbing headlines from the turbulent civil rights era, such as the Kent State shootings and the assassination of Martin Luther King Jr. The effect is striking. The contrast between the horrific events of the day and the utter calm of the nativity scene in the song lyrics makes the violence in the news all the more senseless and shocking, and perhaps underscores our impulse to see innocent people slain as martyrs in a larger movement.

A great deal of contemporary music blends music and spoken words. Since this sort of collaboration is at the heart of rap, for example, many students are already highly interested in and somewhat expert at mixing words and music. Consider the enormous popularity of such artists as Eminem, who samples the Aerosmith song "Sing for the Moment" while he raps of being fatherless, or Nas, rapping about the unlimited potential of children over Beethoven's "Für Elise." Most of my students have been listening to songs that mix spoken-word performance with music for most of their lives.

Still, the first time I introduced this exercise, there was some panic in the room. A few kids came up to me right away and said they couldn't play instruments; the assignment wasn't fair. But they were soon calmed with the reassurance that they only needed to play a recording while reading a poem out loud.

The class asked me—and I accepted—to go first. I purposely chose an odd pairing, a Robert Hayden poem titled "The Great Names of Jazz," which I read to a Modern Jazz Quartet recording, *Blues on Bach.* I chose wordless music to avoid the clash of spoken words against spoken words; I wanted to make sure my reading could be heard. I also wanted to pick a piece of music that would be unfamiliar to most of my students. After I finished, the class offered some tepid praise, and then one boy said, "I could do that." It was perfect entrée: "You're next," I told him.

I told kids the rules would be simple: just try some kind of pairing and have some reason for making the choice. Students' choices ranged from the ironic (one boy chose an Orval Lund poem called "wrist-wrestling father," about a son's admiration of his father, while the corny Randy Newman score from Roy Hobbes's home run swing in *The Natural* undercuts the testimony; at the end, the music crescendoed with the line "But I've never been more amazed / Than when I slapped my father's arm down to the table") to the serious and straightforward (one student read a Paul Celan poem about the Holocaust while playing a haunting Samuel Barber violin recording in the background).

As with in-class readings, I ask students to applaud each effort. Then we talk about things we liked about the reading or the pairing of words and music before we consider ways to improve the piece. Since everyone gets a chance to perform, everyone gets a chance to open class at least once. On year-end evaluations, students told me that the musical accompaniment helped take pressure off the performance aspect. Many students asked to do a second round of these readings when everyone had gone around once. But, perhaps even more important, this exercise helps students see poetry and music as companions, not competitors. Each discipline can enrich the other.

Performance Art: Poem–Music Collaboration

The second way I combine music and poetry is to join forces with a music teacher at school. When I heard that one of our music teachers already required his students to interpret words through music, I thought, "Why not use the poems my students are writing?" Luckily for me, this teacher was not only receptive to the idea, but he also had a great deal of experience, having assigned the project on a regular basis. At several schools where I have taught, I have found music teachers willing to collaborate on interdisciplinary projects.

We waited until my students had written a dozen or so poems, and then we met to pair up our students. We decided to match nervous students with especially positive and nurturing collaborators. We also purposely tried to move kids out of their comfort zones. So we tried, for example, matching a poet from my class who happened to play classical violin with a composer who leaned toward heavy metal and grunge. The results were usually exciting and often resulted in a work of art far different from anything either collaborator expected.

Because I wanted to have something concrete on which to gauge my students' performances, I asked students to complete a collaboration log, a sort of diary of their responses all the way through the project. Here is the assignment sheet I pass out to students:

Performance Art: Poem–Music Collaboration

Here are the steps you'll need to follow in order to complete the assignment:

1. Choose a poem from your portfolio you are proud of that you'd like to read out loud. You may need to read several aloud in order to test sounds. In order to guide your selection, you might ask yourself these questions: Which are most dramatic? Which are most conversational? Which poems rely most heavily on visual presentation?

2. Make sure the composer, whose name you have been given, has a copy of your poem by _____ (usually three days after the assignment is announced). Also, trade phone numbers and arrange a minimum of three meeting times between now and the end of the project.

3. Since poets have done the early work in this collaboration, it is only fair that the composers get to live with the poem for a little while. Composers should read the poem **aloud** several times. Listen for patterns in sound, punctuation, line and syllable length, mood. Composers should contact poets immediately if any portion of the poem is unclear.

4. Composers should contact you by _____ with an intial draft (usually one week after receiving the poem).

5. Poets will need to keep a log (a sort of diary) explaining what happens at every stage of the creative process—including every meeting. This will let me know what you were thinking, how hard you worked, and what sorts of creative leaps you took. Make sure to respond to the composer's initial setting in words. What was effective? What needs to be changed and why? What assumptions of yours about music, poetry, or collaboration have changed? What new assumptions, if any, do you make?

6. All work needs to be done outside of class, though the music teacher and I are happy to meet with you individually or with your collaborator. We are also happy to facilitate meetings if you wish.

7. The final draft will be due on _____ (usually three weeks after the initial assignment is given). We will meet together in the band room to perform the poems for one another over a period of two days.

The first few times we worked on the project we had kids time their reading to a cassette recording of the music. This worked well, with collaborators deciding between themselves how quickly to read and how loudly to play the music. These issues remained important even after we started doing more technically sophisticated recordings, those in which the reading was embedded in the music.

When students performed their poems with music, we followed the same procedure I've described several times: performance, applause, positive comments, questions, criticism. One of the most interesting discussion topics was whether the music or the poem was foregrounded; in other words, which was the dominant element in the piece. Since the poems were written first, they tended to get more attention, but some projects featured musical introductions or codas or even passages of wordless music interspersed throughout the poem. Many students chose to write about this tension between the words and the music in their collaboration logs. One year the musicians even gave us the additional assignment of writing poems to wordless musical composition samples (one to three minutes long). Perhaps unsurprisingly, these performances foregrounded the music more heavily in the final product.

Here is a sample collaboration log:

1st meeting: I made a copy of my poems and left it on the senior board. I am excited about working with my partner. He seems like someone I should know, and I've heard he's very talented. I hope he likes my poems and that he can find a way to set them to music without too much trouble.

2nd meeting: (via telephone) I called him after a few days. I had initially given him three poems to work on and he chose the two we liked best together. He wanted to work on two poems at the same time. We talked about different styles of music that would fit the poems. Because of Spanish references in my poem, he thought of Spanish guitar. (He plays classical guitar.) I thought that might fit, too.

3rd meeting: (in the music room) He wrote a piece for my first poem, but not for my second. He wanted to try something creative with computerized sounds, synthesizers that would go well with the "magical garden scenery" of my second poem. I really enjoyed what he wrote so far, but I did find it a bit repetitive.

4th meeting: The computers were down, so we decided to extend the Spanish guitar into the second poem. His idea sounded like it would end in a masterpiece or a disaster because his song did not go with the second poem entirely.

5th meeting: I heard the entire piece for the first time and was surprisingly disappointed. I didn't know where I was going, or how to read my own words. I didn't know where to make pauses or how this would all work. I definitely doubted the musical arrangement. I just honestly didn't like the piece and wished we were doing it another way.

6th meeting: (The presentation) I was incredibly nervous about reading this poem in front of the class because I didn't know how to collaborate with the music. We did some test runs, and I even changed some of my words and the ways in which I read certain lines, but I was still scared. Hearing the poem with the music turned all my feelings of disappointment around about the music. My reading was pretty accurate and it all fit perfectly. I thought the collaboration went extremely well, and I appreciated his music a whole lot more when it all went together. I think the music complemented the poem and that the poem, in a way, complemented the music. I really love the way this project turned out.

This log is fairly typical of many collaboration projects. (And I have used it as a model for students in subsequent classes.) The first musical response to the poems is rather literal: Spanish music for Spanish references in the poem; "magical" music for the "magical" references. This is fine, of course, though sometimes putting together disparate elements leads to greater satisfaction. Necessity is the mother of invention, the saying goes, and when the computers go down, these students are led to think of extending Spanish music into language that is decidedly *not* Spanish.

The absolutes this student uses are also typical: the choice between "masterpiece" and "disaster" and the end product that worked "perfectly" might be potential dangers with this assignment. With perfection as a standard of success, it's easy to imagine many students coming away disappointed. But we talk about other ways of measuring success as well. Note how this student reimagines her own language, even rewriting passages. Just as students found reason to revise their work when they published their poetry (see Chapter 9), these poetry–music performances also provide a strong impetus for students to reconsider their writing afresh.

This student is also forced to read her poem in a new way, hearing different stresses and reading at a new pace. What the music teacher and I kept emphasizing was the value of seeing the collaborative effort as an entity separate from either the music or the poem. We told students that if they created a new work of art altogether they should be proud of their accomplishment. In nearly every case, students told us they loved working on the project and that, by working together, they learned more than they had expected about their writing and reading. Furthermore, they came away with the knowledge that poetry and music are not discrete disciplines. Each discipline informs the other, and studying the fields jointly offers students a richer understanding of the ways in which the fields intersect.

The Haiku Project

The success of our poetry and music collaborations has made the idea of crossing into other disciplines much less daunting for me. I have been thrilled and surprised by the number of other teachers who are willing to engage in collaborative projects—as long as the projects hold clear relevance for their classes. I have worked on many interdisciplinary projects over the past decade. As a representative example, I mention one of our most ambitious collaborations, which came to be known as the Haiku Project.

The first step in this project came when a primary school physical education teacher told me about an article she had read in a teaching journal about using haiku as a vehicle to teaching "creative movement" classes. Having heard of my interest in haiku, she wondered if I'd be interested in working on a project with her.

At the same time, I was working on a committee that set out to create links between grades, schools, and disciplines. I had just asked a fourth-grade teacher if she wanted to have her students work on writing poems with my tenth graders. She agreed right away, but we both wondered what kind of poetry might be equally accessible to both younger and older audiences. The fact that the PE teacher worked with fourth graders herself made our choice clear: we would all work on writing and dancing haiku. Since I had already formed a good partnership with the music teacher, we decided to invite his classes as well. We could have poems written jointly by students in different grades that would be interpreted by music and dance students as well.

Another lucky break came when we learned that the fourth-grade art teacher had just started introducing *sumi* (ink on rice paper) painting in her classes. Many Japanese *sumi* painters use their art to interpret haiku (their own or other people's). The result is called *haiga* (a haiku and a picture on the same canvas). This was fantastic, we thought. A very short poem could now be seen through the filter of another discipline: painting.

Why stop there, we wondered. We invited the AP French, Spanish, and German students in on the project as well. These classes were given the difficult challenge of translating the poems into their respective language—an amazing opportunity for them (How do you maintain brevity? How literal should the translations be?) and for us. We especially liked the complications caused by translation; the changes in word sounds and rhythms across languages affected the way the composers and choreographers went about their work.

We teachers met before school, and we rehearsed with our students independently in our classes and jointly during lunch periods. Together we decided on a program. We chose six of the haiku to perform. In each case, the author read the poem once by itself while a slide of the *sumi-e* was projected on the wall behind the performers. The authors read the poem a second time accompanied by music and dancers. Then the poem was presented in different languages. Finally, the author read the English-language version of the poem one last time.

In order to make every student feel appreciated, we hung every haiku and *sumi-e* on the walls of the small gym where we held the performance. Before and after the formal presentation, we played music composed for all twenty-two pieces and invited the audience to walk around listening, looking, and reading. We put on two shows, one in the morning and one in the evening. About seventy-five people attended each performance, most of them relatives, teachers, and entire classes.

As an artistic ensemble, it was one of the best experiences I've had as a teacher. Students were amazed that people actually showed up to watch them perform, and it was beautiful to see students of different ages and from different subject classes working together, using all their talents in a focused pursuit.

Perhaps the most surprising outcome was the friendships that emerged between students of very different ages. The younger students benefited from the leadership and support of the older students. The older students loved being looked up to by younger students. All rose to the challenge, and some of the interschool collaborators remained in touch long after the show.

Anticipation of an audience outside of the classroom helped to focus all of our in-class activities. We would perform not just for ourselves. Instead, we'd work as a team, helping one another perform as best we could. These shows reconfirmed for me the importance of performing outside of class and have led me to arrange public performances outside the classroom with every poetry class I teach.

Reading outside the English Classroom

I'll never forget our school's first poetry reading. When a group of ten seniors asked for some way to wrap up our poetry class, I suggested we ask the library staff if we could hold a public reading during a lunch period. The librarians were thrilled and suggested we hold the reading on Valentine's Day. "Oh great," I thought. "What do they think we'll be reading, greeting card verse, sappy 'Roses are red' poems perhaps?" (Happily, this was not the case.) February 14 happened to be the next open day, and the librarians were excited about hearing purposeful talk in the library rather than the usual chatter that kept other kids from studying.

Even though I knew this would be a low-key reading, I wanted to minimize the pressure on students and make sure the experience was positive and that it boosted their confidence. I figured we would be the entire audience—who would give up their lunch period to attend a poetry reading?—so I asked the librarians if they could stay for the reading. I thought it would be wonderful for students to hear someone outside the classroom praise their work.

We had already tried some reading exercises and some group performance exercises, but it's a big shift to read solo, especially your own work rather than someone else's. It helped that the students were seniors—they had more self-confidence. It also helped that we were there as a class, a team, supporting one another all the way through. And everyone wanted support, so everyone gave support. In more concentrated preparation for the reading, we practiced in class, standing up and reading aloud for one another. We practiced in the library as well because it was a much larger room and our voices didn't carry as far in the new space.

In order to make the event as unthreatening as possible, I wanted to keep it short. I told each student to read two to three poems. Since many of the poems were autobiographical, choosing the poems to read was difficult for some students. They wanted to offer variety and also to showcase their varied interests and feelings. After getting a volunteer to go first (it happened to be a student who had performed in most of the school plays), we spent some time thinking about the order of the poems. While we rehearsed, students jostled the lineup. "Why don't I read my 'car poem' after your 'freedom poem'?" "I don't want to start with a sad poem right after you've read two sad poems."

After our first rehearsal in class, we realized that we knew one another's poems—had heard them and talked about them over the past several weeks—much better than an unfamiliar audience would know them. So I added one final preperformance requirement: a short introduction to the poem before the reading.

Introductions

Poetry readings can tax an audience's attention even when the very best readers are performing the finest poems. When audience members don't have the written words in front of them, poems can bleed into one another without context. We decided it would be useful to share a brief introduction of the poem, or of the poet, to help the audience understand the poem on a single listen. (Likewise, such an introduction might be helpful with the performance exercises discussed in Chapter 11.)

I ask students what kinds of information they would find most helpful in understanding a poem. Generally when poems are introduced in anthologies or textbooks, the introductions are limited to information about prizes won or teaching appointments, not about the actual poems. But which would be more helpful in reading Seamus Heaney's "Mid-Term Break"—that he won the Nobel Prize and taught at Harvard, or that he grew up in Northern Ireland and witnessed firsthand the violent conflicts between Protestants and Catholics? I tell my students to remember, "The audience has never heard the words before. They don't have the words in front of them. They need your help." But I also encourage them to keep their introductions short. As a general rule, I jokingly say, "Your introduction should never be longer than your poem."

In search of writing models, I asked the class to imagine singers who offer brief introductions to songs they are about to sing. I have also used *The Best American Poetry* series, which offers superb introductions by authors commenting on the genesis of their own poems. Sometimes these introductions are more sophisticated and wordy than a performer might employ, but they almost always provide a way into the poem for readers.

Here, for example, is Rodney Jones's introduction to his poem "Ten Sighs from a Sabbatical" in the 2003 volume: "*Ten Sighs* was fun to write, no big ideas just going down the slide in my journal, but something of the spirit of Roethke came into play, and it seemed true enough, so I hung on to it and worked. The 'great man' in part five is Allen Tate, my teacher for a few weeks who was no doubt waxing poetical when he said he loathed and detested poetry" (in Komunyakaa and Lehman 208). Jones prepares us for the poem's diarylike quality by letting us know from whence it sprang. He further decodes the reference to the "great man," which most readers would not have been able to infer. He also prepares us for the irony in Mr. Tate's line about "loathing and detesting poetry," letting us know not to take it at face value.

My students' introductions varied considerably in topic and tone, and in how much they wanted to reveal about themselves or their work. Here are a few examples from our first readings:

> "I wrote this one last week, but it's about my parents' divorce. They split up when I was in third grade, and I've never really talked about it with anyone."

> "I scribbled this poem down during math class instead of listening to the teacher talk about vectors and angles. It's about my first boyfriend."

> "I wrote this one thinking about the phrase 'just deserts.' I recently learned this phrase comes from a 13th century practice of meting out even-handed justice, but I imagined a world in which getting even meant eating just desserts, nothing else."

> "I have bi-polar disorder. This doesn't mean I'm crazy. It just means I have good days and bad days, like everyone, I guess, but a lot more extreme. This is a poem about being bi-polar."

These introductions provide a personal connection between the poet and the audience that otherwise might not exist. With introductions in hand, we were ready.

Showtime

We publicized the event on posters throughout the school, but we still thought no one would come. To our surprise, ten to fifteen other students attended the reading. Some were friends of the readers; some came just to find out what was going on. Others came to study and decided to listen to some poetry instead. After each poem, we applauded, and the students got a wonderful reception. Even people they didn't know before were telling them they liked their poems.

We hadn't given much thought to ending the reading, so we weren't sure what to do after the last poet read. I started to go up to thank people for coming when an audience member said, "Can I read a poem even though I'm not in your class?" "Of course," I said. This student, a budding rapper, read a personal piece in rhymed couplets, especially refreshing since it was different from any of our poems.

As soon as he was finished, another student raised his hand and said, "Can I read something I scribbled down while I was listening to you all read? I'm not sure it's a poem. I don't know what it is." My students and I shared smiles. Throughout our course, we had often talked about definitions of poetry without coming to any hard conclusions. "Of course. We'd love to hear it, whatever it is," I said.

We applauded this student's effort, too. I thanked people for coming and was thanking the librarians who were generously praising the performers when two students who hadn't read came up to me and said, "We should have poetry readings like this every week." "Do you have any idea how much work that would take?" I asked. We could never do this every week. Not even John Ashbery writes fast enough to have that much new material, I thought.

"Well, what about once a month, then?" I thought for a second and then said, "If you guys want to plan the events, I will talk them up in my classes and encourage students and former students to read." The librarians were also excited about the possibilities. We were sold.

At the next reading, forty students showed up, including fifteen who read. Some were students from my classes, but many were students I had never seen or heard from before. The diversity was especially amazing. There were students from every grade level and every social group among the performers and the audience. And they were all accepting of one another's work.

Eventually our definition of poetry expanded. Some kids asked if they could play guitar and sing songs they'd written. Of course. A few brave jazz band members improvised musical responses to spoken-word performances. Great. One girl asked if she could dance a poem. Why not?

The readings continued to grow, peaking at an audience of about sixty people. We decided to try for something special at the end-of—year reading. We rented a reception room and called the reading a "Slam and Jam", a coffeehouse night that included poetry readings and musical performances. The second year "reading" was even bigger, and now the event is an annual tradition at the Chicago Lab school.

Curtain

Throughout this chapter, I demonstrate ways of going beyond the artificial walls—the apparent disconnections—between academic disciplines. Rather than standing as obstacles, disciplines outside of English can help us better produce and understand literature. (Just as poetry can inform one's understanding of other disciplines as well. Consider, for example, the persona poems in Chapter 8.) All of these public performances helped to make our class work more immediate and more purposeful. More important, these public performances allowed students to give voice to their private selves—some of their strongest feelings and most deeply held beliefs.

These ideas are also the underlying principles behind this book. I chose the title *Wordplaygrounds* in part because I like the idea of merging apparently contradictory elements. Too often we think of language (in school settings, anyway) as laborious, something thought about only in school. But many students use language in very sophisticated ways— on the playground, for example—that we never see in school. I think of a student who barely spoke through four years of English classes and who remained a consistently mediocre student throughout high school. Someone recently told me he is now recording his second hip-hop CD and that he is an amazingly nimble freestyle rapper. Likewise, we think of learning as taking place mostly within the confines of school. But both assumptions are wrong. Language can be playful and fun, and we are tremendously impoverished learners indeed if our learning is limited to information we get in school.

The exercises in this book are designed to make students more confident, to help them find their voices (their writing and their speaking voices). I have also tried to live up to the Deweyan ideal of making life in school look like life outside of school. For this reason, I have asked students to do the work of professional writers—writing, revising, publishing, and reading from their work.

I know that few of my students will become professional poets or performers, but that outcome has never really been my goal. My goal is much bigger and more basic: I want my students to love language and to be aware of their own imaginative powers through language. I want them to see how poetry can enrich their everyday lives here, now, and throughout their lives. I would like all of my students to feel what one student anonymously shared on a year-end evaluation:

> I want the world
> To know I am
> Somebody
> With a dream and a song
> And a voice of my own
> To sing with
> You
> Too.

Works Cited

Brainard, Joe. *I Remember.* New York: Penguin, 1995.

Ciardi, John, and Miller Williams. *How Does a Poem Mean?* 2nd ed. Boston: Houghton Mifflin, 1975.

Cisneros, Sandra. *The House on Mango Street.* New York: Vintage, 1989.

Dewey, John. *Art as Experience.* New York: Minton, Balch, 1934.

———. *On Education: Selected Writings.* New York: Random House, 1964.

———. *The School and Society; and The Child and the Curriculum.* 1956. Chicago: University of Chicago Press, 1990.

———. *Selected Educational Writings.* London: Heinneman, 1966.

Dove, Rita. "Who's Afraid of Poetry?" *Writer's Digest* (February 1995).

Erikson, Erik H. *The Life Cycle Completed.* New York: Norton, 1997.

Fleischman, Paul. *I Am Phoenix: Poems for Two Voices.* Harper & Row, 1985.

———. *Joyful Noise: Poems for Two Voices.* New York: Harper & Row, 1988.

Gioia, Dana. *Can Poetry Matter? Essays on Poetry and American Culture.* St. Paul, MN: Graywolf, 1992.

Greene, Maxine. *Releasing the Imagination: Essays on Education, the Arts, and Social Change.* San Francisco: Jossey-Bass, 1995.

Hall, Donald. *Their Ancient Glittering Eyes: Remembering Poets and More Poets.* New York: Ticknor & Fields, 1992.

Higginson, William J. comp. *Haiku World: An International Poetry Almanac.* New York: Kodansha, 1996.

Hirsch, Edward. *How to Read a Poem: And Fall in Love with Poetry.* New York: Harcourt Brace.

Janeczko, Paul B. *Poetspeak: In Their Work, about their Work.* Scarsdale, NY: Bradbury, 1983.

Koch, Kenneth. *Wishes, Lies and Dreams: Teaching Children to Write Poetry.* New York: Chelsea House, 1970.

Koch, Kenneth, and Farrell, Kate. *Sleeping on the Wing: An Anthology of Modern Poetry, with Essays on Reading and Writing.* New York: Vintage, 1982.

Komunyakaa, Yusef, and David Lehman. *The Best American Poetry, 2003.* New York: Scribner, 2003

Lee, Charlotte I., and Timothy Gura. *Oral Interpretation.* Boston: Houghton Mifflin, 1987.

Motion: American Poems about Sport. Iowa City: University of Iowa Press, 2001.

Neruda, Pablo. *Odes to Common Things.* Boston: Little, Brown, 1994.

Nye, Naomi Shihab. *What Have You Lost?* New York: Greenwillow, 1999.

O'Brien, Tim. *The Things They Carried.* Boston: Houghton Mifflin, 1990.

Oliver, Mary. *A Poetry Handbook.* San Diego: Harcourt Brace, 1994.

Rosenblatt, Louise M. *Literature as Exploration.* New York: Modern Language Association, 1983.

Rushdie, Salman. *The Ground beneath Her Feet.* New York: Henry Holt, 1999.

Stafford, William. *Writing the Australian Crawl.* Ann Arbor: University of Michigan Press, 1978.

Tsujimoto, Joseph I. *Teaching Poetry Writing to Adolescents.* Urbana, IL: National Council of Teachers of English/ERIC Clearinghouse on Reading and Communication Skills, 1988.

Wilhelm, Jeffrey D. *"You Gotta BE the Book": Teaching Engaged and Reflective Reading with Adolescents.* New York: Teachers College Press, 1997.

Wills, Garry, trans. *Saint Augustine's Memory.* New York: Viking, 2003

Wolff, Tobias. *This Boy's Life.* New York: Grove, 1989.

Wooldridge, Susan G. *poemcrazy: freeing your life with words.* New York: Three Rivers Press, 1997.

Author

Photo by Mike Hill.

John S. O'Connor has an AB in philosophy and English and an MAT (English) from the University of Chicago and has taught English for the past eighteen years in a wide variety of settings (public, parochial, independent, alternative schools; a maximum security prison; an adult literacy agency) and at every level from sixth grade to college, including three years at Penn State University and ten at the University of Chicago Laboratory Schools. He currently teaches at New Trier High School outside of Chicago. O'Connor has written on English and interdisciplinary education in periodicals such as *English Journal, Shakespeare,* and *OAH Magazine of History* and has presented at local and national conferences. His poetry has appeared in journals such as *Rhino, Penumbra,* and *Frogpond* and in *Room Full of Chairs,* a book of haiku. O'Connor is also a folksinger and has set poems of well-known poets to music on a CD titled *Evenings and Other Beginnings.* He has performed at the Chicago Humanities Festival, the Phoenix Writers Workshop, and many other arts festivals and libraries, and his music has been featured on WBEZ radio and on the WLS Sunday morning television program.

This book was typeset in Palatino and Helvetica by Electronic Imaging.
Typefaces used on the cover include Arquitectura and Frutiger.
The book was printed on 60-lb. Williamsburg Offset paper by Versa Press, Inc.